THE GREAT TREKS OF THE WORLD

Trekking the CORSICA GR20

by Andrew McCluggage

KNIFE EDGE Outdoor Guidebooks

About the Author

Andrew McCluggage is an outdoor writer and photographer from Northern Ireland. After 20 years as a corporate lawyer, he decided to do something interesting and started writing walking guidebooks.

His first book was Walking in the Briançonnais, a beautiful part of the French Alps. Since then, he has written a variety of guidebooks for hiking and trekking.

Other Knife Edge Outdoor Guidebooks written by Andrew include:

- Tour du Mont Blanc
- Trekking the Dolomites AV1
- Walker's Haute Route: Chamonix to Zermatt
- Trekking the Tour of the Écrins
- Trekking the Mallorca GR221
- Trekking Iceland's Laugavegur Trail
- Trekking the West Highland Way
- Trekking the Hadrian's Wall Path
- Trekking the Coast to Coast Path
- Trekking the Cotswold Way
- Trekking the Cleveland Way
- Trekking the South Downs Way
- Walking Chamonix-Mont Blanc
- Walking Brittany
- Northern Ireland: the Unmissable Walks
- The Mourne Mountains
- Big Hikes in the Mourne Mountains

Climbing above Bocca di Pisciaghia (Stage 2)

KNIFE EDGE Outdoor Guidebooks

Publisher: Knife Edge Outdoor Limited (NI648568)
12 Torrent Business Centre, Donaghmore, County Tyrone, BT70 3BF, UK
www.knifeedgeoutdoor.com

ISBN: 978-1-912933-61-7

First edition 2021
Second edition 2025

A catalogue record for this book is available from the British Library.

Front cover: Lac de Nino (Stage 6a)

Title page: Magnificent scenery on Stage 6a

This page: Lac de Capitello (Stage 7)

Contents

All routes described in this guide have been recently walked by the author and both the author and publisher have made all reasonable efforts to ensure that all information is as accurate as possible. However, while a printed book remains constant for the life of an edition, things in the countryside often change. Trails are subject to forces outside our control: for example, landslides, tree-falls or other matters can result in damage to paths or route changes; waymarks and signposts may fade or be destroyed by wind, snow or the passage of time; or trails may not be maintained by the relevant authorities. If you notice any discrepancies between the contents of this guide and the facts on the ground, then please let us know. Our contact details can be found at the back of this book.

Getting Help

Emergency Services Number: **dial 112**

Distress Signal

The signal that you are in distress is 6 blasts on a whistle spaced over a minute, followed by a minute's silence. Then repeat. The acknowledgment that your signal has been received is 3 blasts of a whistle over a minute followed by a minute's silence. At night, flashes of a torch can also be used in the same sequences. **Always carry a torch and whistle.**

Signalling to a Helicopter from the Ground

Help Required

Raise both arms in the shape of a 'Y'

Help Not Required

Raise one arm and extend the other arm down and outwards

WARNING

Hills and mountains can be dangerous places and walking is a potentially dangerous activity. Many of the routes described in this guide cross exposed and potentially hazardous terrain. You walk entirely at your own risk. It is solely your responsibility to ensure that you and all members of your group have adequate experience, fitness and equipment. Neither the author nor the publisher accepts any responsibility or liability whatsoever for death, injury, loss, damage or inconvenience resulting from use of this book, participation in the activity of mountain walking or otherwise.

Some land may be privately owned so we cannot guarantee that there is a legal right of entry to the land. Occasionally, routes change as a result of land disputes.

The steep climb approaching Pointe des Éboulis (Stage 4)

Introduction

Clouds forming only on one side of the ridge (Stage 12)

The GR20 is the stuff of legend. Most seasoned trekkers have it on their list of the world's best treks. Those who have walked it never forget it, forever regaling others with tales of their exploits. Few other treks provide so many talking points. And few other treks instil in the walker such a complicated mixture of emotions: joy, exhilaration and awe coexist with respect, fear and intimidation. And it is fair to say that to complete the GR20 is to achieve something worthwhile and unforgettable. Something that required you to dig deep within yourself. Something to be truly proud of.

The GR20 is a linear trek which travels the long spine of the rugged and spectacular mountain range on the Mediterranean island of Corsica. It is, without a doubt, one of the wildest treks in Europe. The fact that Corsica is also a popular summer holiday island is a complete irrelevance to the GR20 trekker: the impenetrable granite mountains of the interior are far-removed from the coast and once you start on the route, you will not lay eyes on a non-trekking tourist until you finish. Unlike many other European treks, the GR20 stays well away from civilisation, crossing rural roads only a handful of times. Over 200km, only two villages are entered: Vizzavona (which offers a welcome opportunity for rest and resupply roughly halfway along the route) and Bavella (at the S end of the trek). Furthermore, cell-phone network is rarely available along the way. The GR20 is a true wilderness experience.

The mountain scenery on the route is exquisite: jagged rocky peaks, sheer cliffs, lofty mountain passes (or 'boccas'), shimmering cobalt lakes and glorious green pastures bedecked with wild-flowers. Nothing can prepare you for the splendour that you will experience. Such beauty is not given away cheaply though: it is no exaggeration to state that the GR20 is one of the hardest treks in Europe (see 'How hard is the GR20?'). The rocky terrain is very challenging, frequently requiring the use of hands and always requiring absolute concentration. Corsica is hot too which saps your energy. Furthermore, such hardships mean that the choice of equipment on the GR20 is more critical than on most other European treks. Itinerary planning too requires more careful thought than usual. Many people fail to complete the GR20 because they carry too much and/or underestimate the difficulties, trying to travel too far each day. Even experienced trekkers can become unstuck.

Despite the challenges, the GR20 is one of the most rewarding of the world's treks. Those who walk it witness scenery accessible to very few. The camaraderie with other trekkers (from all around the world) is wonderful. And the feeling of satisfaction on completion of the trek is something to be savoured.

Lac de Melo (Stage 7)

With this book, we aim to ensure that you have the best chance possible of completing the trek. We place great importance on the correct preparation. We focus in detail on modern, lightweight equipment (see 'Equipment'). And we believe that, on the GR20, it is crucial to match your itinerary to your experience, fitness and ability. Accordingly, we have included here an extraordinary level of detail on itinerary planning: our unique itinerary planner has 15 different itineraries to choose from. For each itinerary, we have completed for you all the difficult calculations of time, distance and altitude gain/loss. And to guide you on the trek itself, we have included real IGN maps (scale: 1:25,000) for each stage.

Ask the Author

If you have any questions which are not answered by this book, then you can ask the author on our Facebook Group, 'Corsica GR20 Q&A'

Basic facts about Corsica

- Corsica is the fourth largest island in the Mediterranean Sea. It sits just off the W coast of Italy.
- Although it is part of France, it has its own unique character and culture.
- It is 183km long and 83km wide. It has approximately 1,000km of coastline.
- The mountains comprise about two-thirds of the island. The highest mountain is Monte Cinto (2706m).
- The population of Corsica is about 330,000.
- Bastia is the capital of Corsica.
- French is the main language but apparently, there are still approximately 30,000 native speakers of the Corsican language (which is related to medieval Tuscan). You will see evidence of the Corsican language on maps and road signs.

How hard is the GR20?

Notwithstanding the challenges, the GR20 is walked by an estimated 20,000 to 30,000 people each year. It is therefore an achievable endeavour. The information below is not intended to discourage: it is intended to provide you with an objective and realistic assessment of the hardships that you will face so that you can determine whether the trek is suitable for you.

The GR20 is a multi-day trek with significant distances to travel, and metres to climb, each day. On paper, the statistics are comparable with many alpine treks such as the Tour du Mont Blanc and the Walker's Haute Route. However, in practice the GR20 is harder. In fact, many consider it to be one of the hardest treks in Europe and it has a high failure rate. In France, it has a legendary reputation and is often viewed as a kind of 'rite of passage'. Even the French Foreign Legion train on the route.

A good level of fitness is required to complete the GR20 which is physically and mentally challenging. A sure foot and a head for heights are also essential. Although not absolutely necessary, previous experience of backpacking and camping will help. Furthermore, it is advisable to train well for the trek: there is no substitute for training walks, carrying a pack. Although some inexperienced trekkers complete the GR20, it is better suited to the experienced walker.

There are five key reasons why the GR20 is considered to be one of the hardest in Europe:

Terrain: the rocky terrain is very challenging, particularly on the northern half of the route. It is relentless, throwing up new challenges day after day. Large sections of the trek have no path. Frequently, you must cross long sections of boulders. There is much scrambling too and you will frequently need to use your hands. Often the step up from one boulder to the next is large, putting great strain on your leg muscles and sapping your energy.

You will travel more slowly than normal, covering smaller distances than you are used to. In fact, some stages are so difficult that distance has little relevance at all: forget about your normal walking speed and focus more on the times given for each stage. The terrain on the GR20 is so different from what most trekkers are used to, that it is easy to overestimate the distance that you will be able to travel in a day. This leads to planning errors: trekkers often bite off more than they can chew, leaving them exhausted and sometimes unable to continue.

A mistake on such difficult terrain can result in serious injury so you must concentrate carefully at all times, forever focusing on where you place your feet and looking out for the next waymark. Such a high level of concentration further saps your energy.

Fortunately, the challenge is mitigated slightly by the fact that much of the rock is granite which provides excellent grip. However, in wet conditions it can still be slippery. The excellent waymarking helps too: in fact there are few treks in the world which have better waymarking than the GR20.

Exposure: many sections of the route are very exposed with steep drops. A fall could be serious causing injury or even death. This adds to the mental challenge and the GR20 is not a place for those who have a fear of heights.

Climate: in trekking season, the sun in Corsica can be brutal. The high temperatures sap your energy and there is little shade. Many will not have trekked in such hot conditions before and some find it to be oppressive. The climate further reduces the distance that you can cover each day. De-hydration and sunstroke are possibilities and you must carry more water than normal: water is heavy and this adds to your burden. Furthermore, in high summer, afternoon thunderstorms occur frequently.

Remoteness: once you start the trek, you will not see civilisation again until Vizzavona which is roughly halfway. As the route crosses roads only a handful of times, medical assistance usually requires a mountain rescue helicopter. To compound the sense of isolation, cell-phone network is rarely available on the GR20. There may be reception at some high points along the trail but this is the exception rather than the rule. In the modern world, many find this to be uncomfortable but others embrace it, recognising a rare opportunity to get away from calls and emails.

Equipment: you will need to carry more than on other European treks. Even if you stay in refuges or fixed tents, you will still need to bring a sleeping bag. And because the refuges on the GR20 are small and book up quickly, most trekkers bring their own camping equipment. On a normal trek, it is difficult enough to carry camping gear but on the GR20, the burden of the extra weight is magnified by the challenges of the terrain and the climate. It is fair to say that most trekkers set off carrying equipment which is unnecessary or simply too heavy: this often results in injury and/or exhaustion, leading to abandonment. Of the five difficulties discussed here, this is the only one that you have any control over. You should therefore give equipment choice careful consideration: it will be crucial to your enjoyment of the trek and the likelihood of success.

Direction and start/finish points

The GR20 runs between Calenzana in the N and Conca in the S. Traditionally, it is walked N to S and the vast majority travel that way. However, an increasing number of walkers now tackle it S to N and there are some compelling reasons why that approach makes better sense. Firstly, the S half of the trek is generally easier than the N half: the four most northerly stages (Stages 1 to 4) are some of the toughest and they make for a brutal introduction to the trek. Many starting in the N find that they are exhausted after a few days. However, those starting in the S have an easier start, only reaching the most exposed and difficult sections towards the end of the trek, by which time the body has adjusted physically to the rigours of the trail and the mind is better prepared for the more serious exposure and difficulty.

Secondly, although the S half of the trek is visually stunning, the N section is even more spectacular. By walking S-N, you save the best for last. Thirdly, some prefer not to meet the same people every day and walking against the flow alleviates this. Fourthly, snow lies later on the high sections of the N half of the GR20: accordingly, in early June, it can be advantageous to start in the S to allow further time for the snow on the high passes in the N to melt.

In this book we cater for both N-S and S-N trekkers: a variety of itineraries are given for both approaches. Although the stage introductions are written from the perspective of a N-S trekker, full route descriptions are provided for both N-S and S-N routes. The real maps in this book, with numbered waypoints, make the route descriptions simple to follow in either direction.

It is also possible to walk shorter sections of the GR20. The village of Vizzavona is roughly halfway along the route and is connected to the main Corsican cities by train. Accordingly, many people walk just the N half or the S half of the trek. There are also a number of escape/access points along the route where you could leave or join the trek using public transport or taxis: see 'On the Trail'. You could start at any of these places and walk a few sections. Or you could skip sections by leaving the route at one of these points.

Guided tours, self-guided tours or independent walking?

A frequently asked question is whether to walk independently or with a guided group. The answer is a personal one, depending upon your own particular circumstances and requirements. For many, the decision to organise the trek themselves, and to walk independently, can be almost life-changing, opening the door for other challenges in the future. There is much satisfaction to be gained in planning and navigating a trek yourself and the sense of achievement on completion is to be savoured.

However, the independent trekker usually carries his own pack and is responsible for all daily decisions such as pacing; which way to go at junctions; when to stock up with food and water; and choice of route in bad weather. For some, this will be too great a burden on top of the physical effort required simply to walk the route. For those walkers, a guided group is a great solution: the tour company typically organises food, accommodation and (if possible) transfer of luggage each night. And the guide makes all the decisions, enabling the walker to concentrate on the walking. There are a number of tour companies operating guided trips on the GR20 but some do not cover the full official route.

Self-guided tours are a popular middle-ground. The tour company books all the accommodation and provides all the advice and information required to complete the

The lovely grassy terrain on Stage 6a

trek. Often they will also arrange your food. However, the trekker walks the trail without a guide and normally (but not always) carries his/her own pack.

Some tour companies (guided and self-guided) offer luggage transfers, delivering your bags to fixed points along the trail. However, the geography of the GR20 dictates that you will only be able to get your bags delivered to certain overnight stops which have road access: normally, Haut Asco, Castel de Vergio, Vizzavona, Capannelle, Col de Verde, Bergerie de Croci and Bavella. You would have to carry your gear yourself for the other overnight stops.

Many confident trekkers (who would be perfectly capable of walking independently) book a self-guided trip simply to avail of the accommodation booking service. By booking a self-guided tour, the stress and hassle are alleviated, albeit at a price.

When to go

Normally you can tackle the GR20 from June to mid-October. Between mid-June and mid-September, refuges are likely to be full so book early if you want a dormitory bed or fixed tent.

June is probably the best time to trek the GR20, as soon as the snow has cleared from the paths. The days are long and the weather is normally warm and sunny: temperatures increase as the month progresses. The peaks are very photogenic, often still frosted with snow. Summer haze has not yet arrived so visibility is generally excellent with wide-ranging views. The summer thunderstorms, for which Corsica is famous, are less likely. And there are carpets of spring wild-flowers. Of course, there is occasionally rain at this time of year but this usually lessens as the month progresses. At the start of the month, there are fewer trekkers and the mountains are more peaceful. However, by the middle of the month, the trek is busy. The refuges are staffed from the end of May. Most private bergeries will open during the first half of the month. Some public transport may not be available early in the month: check in advance.

In some years, snow lies on high passes until mid-June, making short sections of the GR20 difficult and/or dangerous: in such conditions, crampons and/or an ice-axe might be helpful. There are now some very light and compact crampons available which weigh a mere 300g so carrying them just in case is not the burden it once was. Microspikes are another lightweight option for early-season trekkers.

July/August is the main summer season. All refuges and private bergeries are fully staffed and all public transport should operate. It can be very hot, sometimes reaching well over 30°C. Mornings often start with clear, sunny skies and heat up as the sun gains height. If there is to be cloud or haze, often this will arrive in the afternoon when thunderstorms are more likely. Start walking early in the morning to complete the main climb while the temperature is cooler. This is the busiest time on the GR20 and it is advisable to make bookings for refuges and fixed tents well in advance. Do not turn up without a reservation and expect to find a bed. Some water sources may be dry.

September is the new June! It can be a great month for walking as the weather is often more settled than in summer. Skies are usually clear and visibility excellent. Daytime temperatures are normally still warm but evenings get cooler and the days get shorter. It used to be that the number of trekkers reduced dramatically at the end of August so that the mountains were significantly quieter and there was much less demand for accommodation. Nowadays, with the increased popularity of the GR20, refuges and fixed tents are frequently full to capacity even in September. However, it is still fair to say that the number of trekkers decreases, and bookings become easier, as September progresses.

Nevertheless, it is still wise to book in advance. During the month, private bergeries may close for the season and some bus services may cease to operate. Some water sources may be dry.

October is the end of the trekking season and is probably the quietest time on the GR20. Sometimes the autumn weather can be magnificent: clear skies and warm sunny days. However, there is a greater chance of rain and the likelihood of snow on the high passes increases as the month progresses. Evenings can be cold with frost at altitude. Normally, staff leave the refuges early in the month but they remain open: you can still sleep in the dormitories but there will be no food available. Private bergeries and many shops will be closed so you will need to carry more food and plan carefully. Many bus routes will have stopped operating. In summary, October trekking is best suited to more experienced trekkers.

Month	Pros	Cons
June	Cooler than July/August Frequent sunny skies Good visibility Wild-flower season Fewer visitors in early June	Rainy spells are possible Possibility of snow at altitude Some shops/bergeries are closed in early June Not all public transport operational
July/August	Generally fine weather All shops/bergeries are open All public transport operational	Very hot Sometimes hazy Afternoon thunderstorms Visitor numbers highest
September	Cooler than July/August Frequent sunny skies Excellent visibility Fewer visitors	Shorter days Cooler evenings Some shops/bergeries closed Not all public transport operational
October	Sometimes crisp clear skies Excellent visibility Fewer visitors Autumn colours	Shortest days It can be cold Possibility of snow at altitude Some shops/bergeries are closed Not all public transport operational

Above the clouds on Stage 2

Using this book

This book is designed to be used by walkers of differing abilities. Many guidebooks for long-distance treks rigidly divide the route into a fixed number of long day stages, leaving it up to the walker to break down those stages to design daily routes which suit his/her abilities. This book, however, has been laid out differently to give the trekker flexibility: it divides the route into 23 shorter sub-stages which can be combined to design daily routes to meet your own specific needs.

Each of the 23 sub-stages covers the distance between one accommodation option and the subsequent one. Almost every accommodation option on the entire route is the start/ finish point of a sub-stage. You can choose how many of these sub-stages you wish to walk each day. Each sub-stage has its own route descriptions, route map, elevation profile and beautiful photos.

The labelling of the sub-stages uses a combination of numbers and letters. It is a simple system but requires a little bit of explanation. Firstly, every sub-stage has a number between 1 and 16: each number represents one day of our standard 16-day schedule. As the standard 16-day schedule is broken down into sub-stages, these sub-stages are also given letters (e.g. "6a"). Take a look at the detailed Itinerary Planner below and all should become clear.

The Itinerary Planner includes a range of tables outlining fifteen suggested itineraries of 9, 10, 11, 12, 13, 14, 15 and 16 days. We include itineraries for both N-S and S-N walkers. In each table, the maths have been done for you so there is no need for you to waste time (and mental strength!) working out daily distances, timings and height gain.

Of course, the suggested itineraries are only suggestions. You can shorten or lengthen your day in any number of ways to suit yourself: just decide how many sub-stages you want to walk that day. It is up to you. As there is accommodation at the end of each sub-stage, it is easy to design your own bespoke itinerary and adjust it on the ground as you go along.

For example, day 6 of the standard 16-day route involves walking sub-stages 6a and 6b. But you could decide to extend day 6 by walking sub-stages 6a, 6b and 7 all on the same day. Or you might be tired and decide to shorten your day by walking only sub-stage 6a. With some other guidebooks, you would have to work out how to split stages yourself, involving some complicated maths to plan distances and times going forward. This guide, however, does all the hard mental work for you.

In this book:

Timings are the approximate times required by a reasonably fit and experienced walker to complete a sub-stage. They do not include stoppage time. Do not get frustrated if your own times do not match ours: the difficulty of the terrain on the GR20 means that everyone walks at very different speeds. For example, some confident and experienced hikers proceed quickly across exposed sections of boulders while the more cautious might pick their way across gingerly taking twice the time or more. As you progress through the trek, you will soon learn how your own times compare with those given here and you will adjust your plans accordingly. Remember that distances on the GR20 take longer to cover than on most other treks.

Walking distances are measured in kilometres (km) to match maps and signposts in Continental Europe. One mile equates to 1.6km.

One of the GR20's many rock-pools (Stage 5a)

Ascent/descent numbers are the aggregate of all the altitude gain or loss (measured in metres) on the uphill or downhill sections of a sub-stage. As a rule of thumb, a fit walker climbs 300 to 400m in an hour.

Elevation profiles tell you where the climbs and descents fall on each stage. The profile lines have been deliberately drawn in varying thickness purely for aesthetic purposes. Read the elevations off the top of the lines. S-N walkers should read the profiles right to left.

Place names in brackets in the route descriptions indicate the direction to be followed on signposts. For example, "('Vizzavona')" would mean that you follow a sign for Vizzavona.

Spellings of place names are normally derived from the IGN maps. However, there is often disagreement over how Corsican places are spelt. Accordingly, you may notice different spellings elsewhere.

Real maps are provided for each sub-stage. These are extracts from 1:25,000 scale maps produced by IGN, the French mapping agency. The route of the trek is marked on the maps.

The following abbreviations are used:

GR20	Grande Randonnée 20
PNRC	Parc Naturel Régional de Corse
TL	Turn left
TR	Turn right
SH	Straight ahead
N, S, E and W, etc.	North, South, East and West, etc.
N-S	North to South
S-N	South to North

Approaching Bocca Muzzella (Stage 7)

Itinerary Planner

North to South

Stage	Start	Time (hr)	Km	Ascent (m)	Descent (m)	Max. Altitude (m)
1	Calenzana	6.75	11.9	1496	181	1570
2	Refuge de l'Ortu di u Piobbu	6.75	8.2	770	1070	2020
3	Refuge de Carrozzu	5.75	6.1	819	667	1974
4	Haut Asco	7.75	9.4	1265	1004	2607
5a	Refuge Tighiettu	0.50	1.3	0	243	1683
5b	Auberge U Vallone	3.50	6.2	716	165	2041
5c	Refuge Ciuttulu di i Mori	3.50	9.1	125	712	1991
6a	Castel de Vergio	5.75	15.3	566	349	1883
6b	Bergeries de Vaccaghia	0.75	2.0	40	60	1621
7	Refuge de Manganu	6.75	9.3	862	621	2225
8	Refuge de Petra Piana	4.75	10.9	440	897	1842
9	l'Onda	6.00	11.9	751	1216	2115
10	Vizzavona	5.50	15.0	992	326	1641
11a	Capannelle	5.00	14.1	412	709	1631
11b	Col de Verde	2.25	5.1	587	56	1856
12	Refuge de Prati	5.75	11.3	773	843	1981
13a	Refuge d'Usciolu	3.75	9.6	301	736	1834
13b	Bergeries de Basseta	0.75	2.0	105	10	1410
14a	Refuge de Matalza	1.00	3.1	155	15	1550
14b	Bergerie de Croci	3.50	7.5	488	502	2025
15	Refuge d'Asinau	5.00	12.0	422	775	1536
16a	Bavella Village	1.75	4.8	231	359	1206
16b	Refuge d'I Paliri	5.25	13.6	399	1202	1055
Finish	Conca					

Stage 12 involves a fabulous ridge walk

South to North

Stage	Start	Time (hr)	Km	Ascent (m)	Descent (m)	Max. Altitude (m)
16b	Conca	6.50	13.6	1202	399	1055
16a	Refuge d'I Paliri	2.00	4.8	359	231	1206
15	Bavella Village	5.50	12.0	775	422	1536
14b	Refuge d'Asinau	3.50	7.5	502	488	2025
14a	Bergerie de Croci	0.75	3.1	15	155	1550
13b	Refuge Matalza	0.50	2.0	10	105	1410
13a	Bergeries de Bassetta	4.50	9.6	736	301	1834
12	Refuge d'Usciolu	6.00	11.3	843	773	1981
11b	Refuge de Prati	1.75	5.1	56	587	1856
11a	Col de Verde	5.50	14.1	709	412	1631
10	Capanelle	4.75	15.0	326	992	1641
9	Vizzavona	7.00	11.9	1216	751	2115
8	l'Onda	5.50	10.9	897	440	1842
7	Refuge de Petra Piana	6.25	9.3	621	862	2225
6b	Refuge de Manganu	0.75	2.0	60	40	1621
6a	Bergeries de Vaccaghia	5.25	15.3	349	566	1883
5c	Castel de Vergio	4.25	9.1	712	125	1991
5b	Refuge Ciuttulu di i Mori	3.00	6.2	165	716	2041
5a	Auberge U Vallone	0.75	1.3	243	0	1683
4	Refuge Tighiettu	7.25	9.4	1004	1265	2607
3	Haut Asco	5.25	6.1	667	819	1974
2	Refuge de Carrozzu	6.75	8.2	1070	770	2020
1	Refuge de l'Ortu di u Piobbu	5.25	11.9	181	1496	1570
Finish	Calenzana					

Suggested Itineraries: North to South

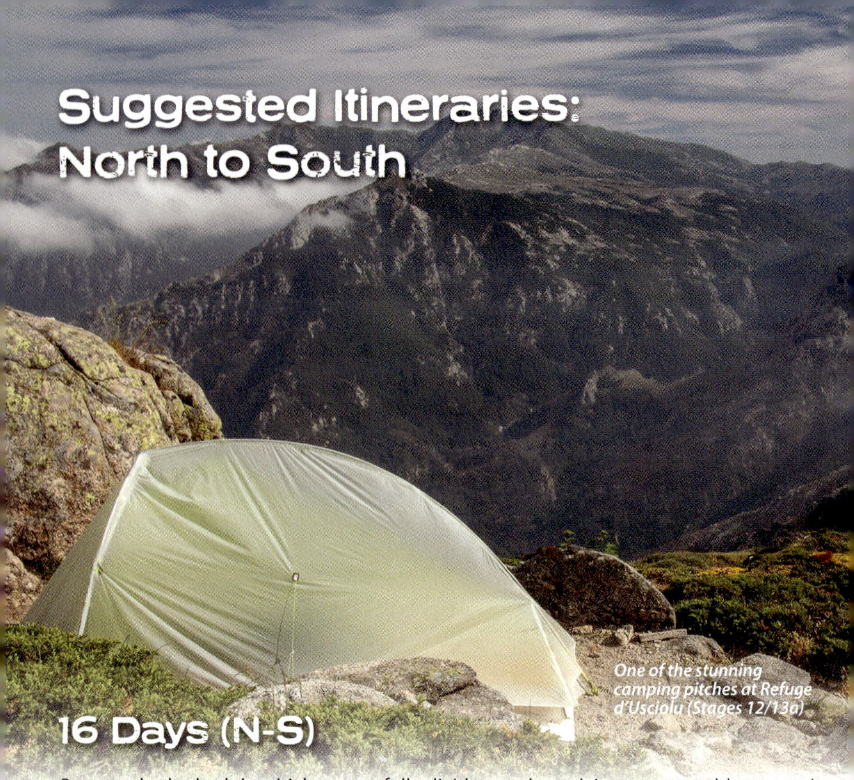

One of the stunning camping pitches at Refuge d'Usciolu (Stages 12/13a)

16 Days (N-S)

Our standard schedule which successfully divides up the trek into manageable stages. It is a tried and tested approach which is suitable for many walkers. Day 1 involves a long, steep climb but there is no way around that.

Day	Stages	Time (hr)	Km	Ascent (m)	Descent (m)
1	1	6.75	11.9	1496	181
2	2	6.75	8.2	770	1070
3	3	5.75	6.1	819	667
4	4	7.75	9.4	1265	1004
5	5a, 5b, 5c	7.50	16.6	841	1120
6	6a, 6b	6.50	17.3	606	409
7	7	6.75	9.3	862	621
8	8	4.75	10.9	440	897
9	9	6.00	11.9	751	1216
10	10	5.50	15.0	992	326
11	11a, 11b	7.25	19.2	999	765
12	12	5.75	11.3	773	843
13	13a, 13b	4.50	11.6	406	746
14	14a, 14b	4.50	10.6	643	517
15	15	5.00	12.0	422	775
16	16a, 16b	7.00	18.4	630	1561

15 Days (N-S)

Days 13, 14 and 15 of the 16-day itinerary are squeezed into two days. The first twelve stages remain the same.

Day	Stages	Time (hr)	Km	Ascent (m)	Descent (m)
1	1	6.75	11.9	1496	181
2	2	6.75	8.2	770	1070
3	3	5.75	6.1	819	667
4	4	7.75	9.4	1265	1004
5	5a, 5b, 5c	7.50	16.6	841	1120
6	6a, 6b	6.50	17.3	606	409
7	7	6.75	9.3	862	621
8	8	4.75	10.9	440	897
9	9	6.00	11.9	751	1216
10	10	5.50	15.0	992	326
11	11a, 11b	7.25	19.2	999	765
12	12	5.75	11.3	773	843
13	13a, 13b, 14a	5.50	14.7	561	761
14	14b, 15	8.50	19.5	910	1277
15	16a, 16b	7.00	18.4	630	1561

14 Days (N-S)

Days 10, 11 and 12 of the 15-day itinerary are squeezed into two days. The first nine stages remain the same. Day 10 is very long.

Day	Stages	Time (hr)	Km	Ascent (m)	Descent (m)
1	1	6.75	11.9	1496	181
2	2	6.75	8.2	770	1070
3	3	5.75	6.1	819	667
4	4	7.75	9.4	1265	1004
5	5a, 5b, 5c	7.50	16.6	841	1120
6	6a, 6b	6.50	17.3	606	409
7	7	6.75	9.3	862	621
8	8	4.75	10.9	440	897
9	9	6.00	11.9	751	1216
10	10, 11a	10.50	29.1	1404	1035
11	11b, 12	8.00	16.4	1360	899
12	13a, 13b, 14a	5.50	14.7	561	761
13	14b, 15	8.50	19.5	910	1277
14	16a, 16b	7.00	18.4	630	1561

13 Days (N-S)

Days 8 and 9 of the 14-day itinerary are squeezed into one day: this is a very long walk. The first 7 stages remain the same. For fit walkers only.

Day	Stages	Time (hr)	Km	Ascent (m)	Descent (m)
1	1	6.75	11.9	1496	181
2	2	6.75	8.2	770	1070
3	3	5.75	6.1	819	667
4	4	7.75	9.4	1265	1004
5	5a, 5b, 5c	7.50	16.6	841	1120
6	6a, 6b	6.50	17.3	606	409
7	7	6.75	9.3	862	621
8	8, 9	10.75	22.8	1191	2113
9	10, 11a	10.50	29.1	1404	1035
10	11b, 12	8.00	16.4	1360	899
11	13a, 13b, 14a	5.50	14.7	561	761
12	14b, 15	8.50	19.5	910	1277
13	16a, 16b	7.00	18.4	630	1561

12 Days (N-S)

Days 10 to 12 of the 13-day itinerary are squeezed into two days. Days 8 to 11 are all very long. The first seven stages remain the same. For fit walkers only.

Day	Stages	Time (hr)	Km	Ascent (m)	Descent (m)
1	1	6.75	11.9	1496	181
2	2	6.75	8.2	770	1070
3	3	5.75	6.1	819	667
4	4	7.75	9.4	1265	1004
5	5a, 5b, 5c	7.50	16.6	841	1120
6	6a, 6b	6.50	17.3	606	409
7	7	6.75	9.3	862	621
8	8, 9	10.75	22.8	1191	2113
9	10, 11a	10.50	29.1	1404	1035
10	11b, 12, 13a	11.75	26.0	1661	1635
11	13b, 14a, 14b, 15	10.25	24.6	1170	1302
12	16a, 16b	7.00	18.4	630	1561

11 Days (N-S)

Days 4 to 7 of the 12-day itinerary are squeezed into three days. Days 4, 5, 7, 8, 9 and 10 are all very long. The first three stages remain the same. For very fit walkers only.

Day	Stages	Time (hr)	Km	Ascent (m)	Descent (m)
1	1	6.75	11.9	1496	181
2	2	6.75	8.2	770	1070
3	3	5.75	6.1	819	667
4	4, 5a	8.25	10.7	1265	1247
5	5b, 5c, 6a	12.75	30.6	1407	1226
6	6b, 7	7.50	11.3	902	681
7	8, 9	10.75	22.8	1191	2113
8	10, 11a	10.50	29.1	1404	1035
9	11b, 12, 13a	11.75	26.0	1661	1635
10	13b, 14a, 14b, 15	10.25	24.6	1170	1302
11	16a, 16b	7.00	18.4	630	1561

10 Days (N-S)

Days 2 and 3 of the 11-day itinerary are squeezed into one day. The first two days are a brutal introduction to the trek: you will need to be in good shape before starting. Almost every day is a long one. For very fit walkers only.

Day	Stages	Time (hr)	Km	Ascent (m)	Descent (m)
1	1	6.75	11.9	1496	181
2	2, 3	12.50	14.3	1589	1737
3	4, 5a	8.25	10.7	1265	1247
4	5b, 5c, 6a	12.75	30.6	1407	1226
5	6b, 7	7.50	11.3	902	681
6	8, 9	10.75	22.8	1191	2113
7	10, 11a	10.50	29.1	1404	1035
8	11b, 12, 13a	11.75	26.0	1661	1635
9	13b, 14a, 14b, 15	10.25	24.6	1170	1302
10	16a, 16b	7.00	18.4	630	1561

9 Days (N-S)

Tough and relentless from start to finish: you will need to be in very good shape before starting. Every day is a long one. For very fit walkers only.

Day	Stages	Time (hr)	Km	Ascent (m)	Descent (m)
1	1	6.75	11.9	1496	181
2	2, 3	12.50	14.3	1589	1737
3	4, 5a	8.25	10.7	1265	1247
4	5b, 5c, 6a, 6b	13.50	32.6	1447	1286
5	7, 8	11.50	20.2	1302	1518
6	9, 10	11.50	26.9	1743	1542
7	11a, 11b, 12	13.00	30.5	1772	1608
8	13a, 13b, 14a, 14b	9.00	22.2	1049	1263
9	15, 16a, 16b	12.00	30.4	1052	2336

Stage 15 is often overlooked but the scenery is wonderful

Suggested Itineraries: South to North

Col d'Avartoli (Stage 2)

16 Days (S-N)

Our standard schedule which successfully divides up the trek into manageable stages. It is a tried and tested approach which is suitable for many walkers. Day 1 involves a long climb but there is no way around that.

Day	Stages	Time (hr)	Km	Ascent (m)	Descent (m)
1	16b	6.50	13.6	1202	399
2	16a, 15	7.50	16.8	1134	653
3	14b, 14a	4.25	10.6	517	643
4	13b, 13a	5.00	11.6	746	406
5	12	6.00	11.3	843	773
6	11b, 11a	7.25	19.2	765	999
7	10	4.75	15.0	326	992
8	9	7.00	11.9	1216	751
9	8	5.50	10.9	897	440
10	7	6.25	9.3	621	862
11	6b, 6a	6.00	17.3	409	606
12	5c, 5b, 5a	8.00	16.6	1120	841
13	4	7.25	9.4	1004	1265
14	3	5.25	6.1	667	819
15	2	6.75	8.2	1070	770
16	1	5.25	11.9	181	1496

15 Days (S-N)

Days 3 and 4 of the 16-day itinerary are squeezed into one day. The last twelve stages remain the same.

Day	Stages	Time (hr)	Km	Ascent (m)	Descent (m)
1	16b	6.50	13.6	1202	399
2	16a, 15	7.50	16.8	1134	653
3	14b, 14a, 13b, 13a	9.25	22.2	1263	1049
4	12	6.00	11.3	843	773
5	11b, 11a	7.25	19.2	765	999
6	10	4.75	15.0	326	992
7	9	7.00	11.9	1216	751
8	8	5.50	10.9	897	440
9	7	6.25	9.3	621	862
10	6b, 6a	6.00	17.3	409	606
11	5c, 5b, 5a	8.00	16.6	1120	841
12	4	7.25	9.4	1004	1265
13	3	5.25	6.1	667	819
14	2	6.75	8.2	1070	770
15	1	5.25	11.9	181	1496

14 Days (S-N)

Days 9 to 12 of the 15-day itinerary are squeezed into three days. Day 11 is very long.

Day	Stages	Time (hr)	Km	Ascent (m)	Descent (m)
1	16b	6.50	13.6	1202	399
2	16a, 15	7.50	16.8	1134	653
3	14b, 14a, 13b, 13a	9.25	22.2	1263	1049
4	12	6.00	11.3	843	773
5	11b, 11a	7.25	19.2	765	999
6	10	4.75	15.0	326	992
7	9	7.00	11.9	1216	751
8	8	5.50	10.9	897	440
9	7, 6b	7.00	11.3	681	902
10	6a, 5c	9.50	24.4	1061	691
11	5b, 5a, 4	11.00	16.9	1412	1981
12	3	5.25	6.1	667	819
13	2	6.75	8.2	1070	770
14	1	5.25	11.9	181	1496

13 Days (S-N)

Days 4, 5 and 6 of the 14-day itinerary are squeezed into two days. Days 3, 5, 9 and 10 are very long. For fit walkers only.

Day	Stages	Time (hr)	Km	Ascent (m)	Descent (m)
1	16b	6.50	13.6	1202	399
2	16a, 15	7.50	16.8	1134	653
3	14b, 14a, 13b, 13a	9.25	22.2	1263	1049
4	12, 11b	7.75	16.4	899	1360
5	11a, 10	10.25	29.1	1035	1404
6	9	7.00	11.9	1216	751
7	8	5.50	10.9	897	440
8	7, 6b	7.00	11.3	681	902
9	6a, 5c	9.50	24.4	1061	691
10	5b, 5a, 4	11.00	16.9	1412	1981
11	3	5.25	6.1	667	819
12	2	6.75	8.2	1070	770
13	1	5.25	11.9	181	1496

12 Days (S-N)

Days 7 to 9 of the 13-day itinerary are squeezed into two days. For fit walkers only.

Day	Stages	Time (hr)	Km	Ascent (m)	Descent (m)
1	16b	6.50	13.6	1202	399
2	16a, 15	7.50	16.8	1134	653
3	14b, 14a, 13b, 13a	9.25	22.2	1263	1049
4	12, 11b	7.75	16.4	899	1360
5	11a, 10	10.25	29.1	1035	1404
6	9	7.00	11.9	1216	751
7	8, 7	11.75	20.2	1518	1302
8	6b, 6a, 5c	10.25	26.4	1121	731
9	5b, 5a, 4	11.00	16.9	1412	1981
10	3	5.25	6.1	667	819
11	2	6.75	8.2	1070	770
12	1	5.25	11.9	181	1496

11 Days (S-N)

Days 10 and 11 of the 12-day itinerary are squeezed into one day: Day 10 is brutally hard. Days 3, 5, 7, 8, and 9 are also very long. For very fit walkers only.

Day	Stages	Time (hr)	Km	Ascent (m)	Descent (m)
1	16b	6.50	13.6	1202	399
2	16a, 15	7.50	16.8	1134	653
3	14b, 14a, 13b, 13a	9.25	22.2	1263	1049
4	12, 11b	7.75	16.4	899	1360
5	11a, 10	10.25	29.1	1035	1404
6	9	7.00	11.9	1216	751
7	8, 7	11.75	20.2	1518	1302
8	6b, 6a, 5c	10.25	26.4	1121	731
9	5b, 5a, 4	11.00	16.9	1412	1981
10	3, 2	12.00	14.3	1737	1589
11	1	5.25	11.9	181	1496

10 Days (S-N)

You will need to be in good shape before starting. Almost every day is a long one. For very fit walkers only.

Day	Stages	Time (hr)	Km	Ascent (m)	Descent (m)
1	16b, 16a	8.50	18.4	1561	630
2	15, 14b, 14a	9.75	22.6	1292	1065
3	13b, 13a, 12	11.00	22.9	1589	1179
4	11b, 11a, 10	12.00	34.2	1091	1991
5	9	7.00	11.9	1216	751
6	8, 7	11.75	20.2	1518	1302
7	6b, 6a, 5c	10.25	26.4	1121	731
8	5b, 5a, 4	11.00	16.9	1412	1981
9	3, 2	12.00	14.3	1737	1589
10	1	5.25	11.9	181	1496

Accommodation

Fixed tents at Refuge de Petra Piana (Stage 7/8)

On the GR20, you can stay in dormitories or fixed tents at refuges. Alternatively, you can pitch your own tent at the permitted campsites at refuges and private bergeries. On rare occasions, there is a gîte or hotel on the route. In addition, there are sometimes gîtes, hotels or campsites a few hours off-route.

Refuges: these form the 'back-bone' of GR20 accommodation. They are run by the PNRC. There is a refuge (or mountain hut) at the end of almost every stage of our standard 16-day itinerary. The huts are usually situated in the heart of the mountains where they are accessible only to walkers. Each refuge has a source of drinking water. The refuges are staffed from the end of May to the start of October. Outside this period, they remain open but are unstaffed.

In season, the refuges offer drinks, breakfast and simple evening meals. Drinks and basic foods (such as cold meats and cheeses) are normally available at lunchtime too. Each refuge also has a small shop where you can buy basic food supplies and fuel: stocks sometimes run out. There will also be a small cooking area where you can prepare your own hot meals: gas cookers, pots/pans, crockery and cutlery are normally provided but the quality and quantity of items varies. Although this means that it is not essential to carry a stove, there are frequently long queues to use the cookers so many prefer to carry their own.

Each refuge normally has a mixed-sex dormitory and fixed tents. Alternatively, you can pitch your own tent nearby: this is what the majority do (see 'Camping' below). The fixed tents are pitched permanently during the season and can normally accommodate up to 2 people. Mattresses are provided in both dormitories and fixed tents but, in each case, you must provide your own sleeping bag. The fixed tents offer more privacy than the dormitories. Toilets and showers are basic and often not very clean. The shower water is solar-heated and may be cold if you arrive later in the day.

The advantage of staying in a refuge is that you do not need to carry camping equipment (other than a sleeping bag). However, there are some disadvantages. Firstly, they are nearly always full to capacity in the trekking season and so they can be quite hectic. Secondly, because the huts are so popular, bookings must be made well in advance: do not expect to find a bed if you turn up without a booking. Thirdly, because refuges need to be booked in advance, it is rarely possible to alter your plans once on the trek. Lastly, bed-bugs are a frequent problem at the refuges: in the fixed tents, you can avoid this issue by bringing your own camping mattress.

On the whole, GR20 refuges are very different to those found in the Alps. They are more basic and standards of cleanliness tend to be lower. The quality of the food is frequently lower too. Bed-bugs are a key reason why many do not stay in refuges, preferring to carry their own tent.

To reserve a place in a refuge dormitory/fixed tent, book online at **www.pnr-resa.corsica**. You will need to pay upfront. Print confirmations and carry them with you. For changes/cancellations to bookings, see 'Camping' below.

When the refuges are unstaffed, you can still sleep in the dormitories but there will be no food available. No reservations are necessary: it is first come, first served.

Communal cooking facilities

Private Bergeries: there are many small farms (or 'bergeries') along the GR20. Some simply sell meals or basic foods (including delicious home-made cheese and cured meats). However, many permit camping too. Because they are privately owned, they tend to be well maintained and are often lovely places to spend some time. Costs of camping and eating at bergeries are usually slightly higher than at PNRC refuges. However, in our opinion, the higher price is worth paying as quality and service are better at bergeries than many refuges. You are unlikely to find communal cooking facilities at the bergeries.

Gîtes d'étape: traditionally, a gîte would have been comparable to a youth hostel, offering beds in dormitories and evening meals. These days, gîtes are often more upmarket: private rooms are sometimes available and the food is usually good. Most gîtes now have their own websites.

Hotels: there are a few hotels along the GR20: Calenzana, Haut Asco, Castel de Vergio, Vizzavona and Conca. They are expensive but can provide a welcome break from camping. As with other accommodation on the GR20, book ahead.

Camping: the majority of trekkers carry their own tents and camp at the designated sites beside refuges and bergeries. In high season, there can be a few hundred tents pitched beside each refuge on any given night. On arrival at the refuge/bergerie, you simply check in with the gardien and then select one of the available pitches. Until 2023, a reservation was not required to camp at PNR refuges: it was first come, first served. However, in 2023, advance booking of camping pitches was made compulsory and this was extended into 2024: currently, you need to book online 48 hours before your day of arrival (**www.pnr-resa.corsica**). If you turn up without a booking, it is unlikely that you will be turned away (if space is available) but you will have to pay a higher fee (about double): however, these days the campsites are very busy so there is always a risk that there will be no space. Unfortunately, this new system puts an end to the blissful flexibility that campers traditionally enjoyed on the GR20. Furthermore, it raises the question (to which there is no clear answer) as to what happens if you get delayed due to bad weather or you need a rest day due to exhaustion. Changes to bookings can be made by emailing or calling PNR at least 2 days before the date of your booking: contact@pnr.corsica; +33 (0)4 20 06 12 00/95 51 79 06. Alternatively, changes can be agreed directly with the gardiens on the ground (only if space permits). Bookings can be cancelled without charge if notified by email at least one month before the start of your trek.

The risk of bush-fires is high so wild camping is prohibited: you are only permitted to camp at the designated camp-grounds. If you get caught breaking the rules, you could face a stiff fine. Wherever you camp, always take your rubbish with you. If nature calls while on the trail, bury your toilet waste away from watercourses and pack-out your toilet paper. Leave no trace.

A typical fixed tent

Camping Pros	Camping Cons
▶ **Cost**: bringing your own tent is cheaper than staying in refuge dormitories/fixed tents ▶ **Flexibility**: you do not need to book in advance ▶ **Privacy and cleanliness**: it is much more pleasant sleeping in your own tent which will be cleaner than the mattresses and tents provided by the refuges. Your own tent should also be bed-bug free!	▶ **Weight**: camping gear adds weight to your pack which makes the trek more difficult ▶ **Comfort**: many of the pitches are hard and rocky so a good mattress is advisable. Many are also sloped which does not provide the best night's sleep. The best pitches are snagged by those who arrive early in the day

A typical refuge dormitory

Accommodation Listings

DB	Dormitory Bed
PR	Private Room
(tent icon)	Camping
(boxed tent icon)	Fixed Tents
(glass icon)	Drinks
(fork and knife icon)	Lunch/Evening Meals
(croissant icon)	Breakfast
(cart icon)	Food shop
(swimmer icon)	Swimming Pool

Rock-pools on Stage 13a

Stage N-S	Name	Beds	Other Facilities	Contact Details
Start/Finish (Calenzana)	Gîte Municipal de Calenzana	30 DB	Camping	+33 (0)4 95 62 77 13
Start/Finish (Calenzana)	Calenzana Camping	-	Camping	No contact details. Reservation not usually required.
Start/Finish (Calenzana)	Hotel Bel Horizon	12 PR	Breakfast, Drinks	+33 (0)4 95 62 71 72 +33 (0)6 80 10 76 88 bernard.villanova@wanadoo.fr www.calenzana.com
Start/Finish (Calenzana)	Gîte U Mandarinu	4 PR		+33 (0)6 03 81 34 28 umandarinu@gmail.com www.umandarinu.wixsite.com
Start/Finish (Calenzana)	Au Pied des Oliviers	3 PR	Breakfast, Swimming Pool	+33 (0)6 50 23 78 61 chambresdhotes@aupiedsdesoliviers.com www.aupieddesoliviers.com
Start/Finish (Calenzana)	A l'Ombre du Clocher	3 PR	Breakfast, Swimming Pool	+33 (0)6 20 80 18 08 berengerecorse@wanadoo.fr www.ombre-du-clocher.com
1/2	Refuge de l'Ortu di u Piobbu (PNRC)	0	Camping, Fixed Tents, Lunch/Evening Meals, Breakfast, Drinks, Food shop	www.pnr.corsica
2 (off-route: Bonifatu)	Auberge de la Forêt	36 DB 6 PR	Camping, Lunch/Evening Meals, Breakfast, Drinks	+33 (0)6 50 77 56 36 www.auberge-foret-bonifatu.com
2/3	Refuge de Carrozzu (PNRC)	36 DB	Camping, Fixed Tents, Lunch/Evening Meals, Breakfast, Drinks, Food shop	www.pnr.corsica

Stage N-S	Name	Beds	Other Facilities	Contact Details
3/4	Hotel/ Restaurant/ Gîte le Chalet	22 PR 36 DB		+33 (0)4 95 47 81 08 info@hotel-lechalet-asco.com www.hotel-lechalet-asco.com
3/4	Refuge d'Ascu Stagnu (PNRC)	36 DB		www.pnr.corsica
4/5a	Refuge Tighiettu (PNRC)	36 DB		www.pnr.corsica
5a/5b	Auberge U Vallone/ Bergerie de Ballone	0		+33 (0)6 12 03 44 65 www.bergeriedeballonegr20.com
5a (off-route: Albertacce)	Hotel a Sant'Anna	8 PR		+33 (0)6 26 83 22 09
5b/5c	Refuge Ciuttulu di i Mori (PNRC)	30 DB		www.pnr.corsica
5c	Bergerie de Radule	0	(not always available)	None
5c/6a	Hotel Castel de Vergio	29 PR		+33 (0)6 12 74 87 04 info@casteldevergio.com www.hotel-castel-vergio.com
5c/6a	Refuge de Castel de Vergio	70 DB		+33 (0)6 12 74 87 04 info@casteldevergio.com www.hotel-castel-vergio.com
6a/6b	Bergeries de Vaccaghia	0	Sells cheese	+33 (0)6 89 35 97 80 Facebook: @donatimariecharlotte
6b/7	Refuge de Manganu (PNRC)	30 DB		www.pnr.corsica
7/8/v8	Refuge de Petra Piana (PNRC)	25 DB		www.pnr.corsica
8	Bergeries de Tolla	1 PR		None
8 (off-route: Savaggio)	Camping de Savaggio	0		+33 (0)6 81 96 08 98 +33 (0)4 95 47 22 14
8 (off-route: Tattone)	Camping le Soleil	0	Free shuttle to/from Vizzavona	+33 (0)4 95 47 21 16 +33 (0)6 64 88 46 16 camping-lesoleil@orange.fr www.camping-lesoleil.fr

Stage N-S	Name	Beds	Other Facilities	Contact Details
8 (off-route: Tattone)	Gîte Chez Pierrot	3 PR		+33 (0)6 24 69 29 85 +33 (0)4 95 31 12 77 www.gite-chez-pierrot.fr
8/v8/9	Refuge de l'Onda (PNRC)	16 DB		www.pnr.corsica
9/10 (Vizzavona)	Hotel/ Restaurant le Vizzavona,	12 PR		+33 (0)4 95 47 21 12 +33 (0)6 72 43 14 42 info@hotel-vizzavona.com www.hotel-vizzavona.com
9/10 (Vizzavona)	L'Alzarella Bivouac	16 DB		www.alzarella.com
9/10 (Vizzavona)	Casa Alta Chambres d'Hôtes	3 PR		+33 0(4) 95 47 21 09 +33 (0)6 72 28 31 46 info@casa-alta.fr www.casa-alta.fr
9/10 (Vizzavona)	Hotel u Castellu	10 PR		+33 (0)4 95 30 53 00 contact@hotel-ucastellu.fr www.hotel-ucastellu.fr
9/10 (Vizzavona)	Le Refuge du GR20	20 DB		+33 (0)4 95 47 22 20 +33 (0)6 24 12 16 27
9/10 (off-route: la Foce)	Gîte/Hotel/ Restaurant Monte d'Oro	40 DB 18 PR		+33 (0)6 14 36 36 07 +33 (0)4 95 47 21 06 monte.oro@vizzavona.fr www.monte-oro.com
9/10 (off-route: la Foce)	La Halte du Prince	DB PR		+33 (0)4 95 46 31 02 +33 (0)6 09 95 63 06 lahalteduprince@gmail.com www.lahalteduprince.com
9/10 (off-route: Tattone)	Camping le Soleil	0	Free shuttle to/from Vizzavona	+33 (0)4 95 47 21 16 +33 (0)6 64 88 46 16 camping-lesoleil@orange.fr www.camping-lesoleil.fr
10/11a	Gîte u Fugone	62 DB		+33 (0)4 95 57 01 81 roger.maurizi@wanadoo.fr www.gite-u-fugone.com
10/11a	Gîte u Renosu	DB		Closed for business at date of press
10/11a	Refuge d'E Capannelle (PNRC)	DB		Online booking not available: enquire at Gîte u Fugone (see above)
11a/11b	Relais San Petru di Verde	DB		+33 (0)4 95 24 46 82 +33 (0)6 74 90 68 62 contact@boccadiverdi.com www.boccadiverdi.com

Stage N-S	Name	Beds	Other Facilities	Contact Details
11b/12	Refuge de Prati (PNRC)	32 DB		www.pnr.corsica
12/13a	Refuge d'Usciolu (PNRC)	31 DB		www.pnr.corsica
13a (off-route: Cozzano)	Le Relais des Cols	3 PR		+33 (0)6 03 74 47 76 lerelaisdescols@gmail.com www.lerelaisdescols.com
13a (off-route: Cozzano)	Auberge a Filetta	PR		+33 (0)6 79 82 37 15
13a/13b (off-route: Zicavo)	Hotel le Florida	PR		+33 0(4) 95 24 43 11 www.hotelleflorida-corse.com
13a/13b (off-route: Zicavo)	Hotel du Tourisme	14 PR		+33 (0)4 95 24 40 06
13a /13b	Bergeries de Basseta	DB		+33 (0)6 76 78 40 48 bassetagr20@gmail.com www.bergerie-de-basseta.fr
13b/14a	Refuge de Matalza	20 DB		contact@refugedematalza.com www.refugedematalza.com
14a/14b	Bergerie de Croci	34 DB		+33 (0)6 89 56 26 52 leandri.louis@gmail.com www.gr20-croci.com
14b/15	Refuge d'Asinau (PNRC)	24 DB		www.pnr.corsica The website does not permit booking of DBs but some may be available on arrival
14b/15	Bergerie d'Asinau - Chez Aline	20 DB		+33 (0)6 17 53 98 92 aline.bologni@sfr.fr Located below the PNRC refuge
15/v15/16a	Gîte les Aiguilles de Bavella, Col de Bavella	40 DB		+33 (0)9 88 11 35 23 www.les-aiguilles-de-bavella.fr
15/v15/16a	Auberge du Col de Bavella, Bavella Village	DB PR		+33 (0)4 95 72 09 87 +33 (0)6 13 14 17 33 auberge.bavella@gmail.com www.auberge-bavella.com
16a/16b	Refuge d'I Paliri (PNRC)	22 DB		www.pnr.corsica

Stage N-S	Name	Beds	Other Facilities	Contact Details
Finish/Start (Conca)	Gîte la Tonnelle	DB PR		+33 (0)4 95 71 46 55 latonnelleconca@hotmail.com www.gite-la-tonnelle.com
Finish/Start (Conca)	Hotel San Pasquale	12 PR		+33 (0)4 95 10 47 30 saparello@orange.fr www.hotelsanpasquale.com

Camping at Refuge d'Asinau (Stage 14b)

Facilities

Stage (N-S)	Place	Dormitory Beds	Fixed Tents	Camping (own tent)	Hotel/ Gîte	Meals/ Drinks	Food Shop	Transport
Start/Finish	Calenzana	✓		✓	✓	✓	✓	✓
1	Refuge de l'Ortu di u Piobbu		✓	✓		✓	✓	
2	Refuge de Carrozzu	✓	✓	✓		✓	✓	
3	Haut Asco	✓	✓	✓	✓	✓	✓	✓
4	Refuge Tighiettu	✓	✓	✓		✓	✓	
5a	Auberge U Vallone		✓	✓		✓	✓	
5b	Refuge Ciuttulu di i Mori	✓	✓	✓		✓	✓	
5c	Castel de Vergio	✓		✓	✓	✓	✓	✓
6a	Bergeries de Vaccaghia			✓		✓		
6b	Refuge de Manganu	✓	✓	✓		✓	✓	
7	Refuge de Petra Piana	✓	✓	✓		✓	✓	
8	l'Onda	✓	✓	✓		✓	✓	

Stage (N-S)	Place	Dormitory Beds	Fixed Tents	Camping (own tent)	Hotel/ Gîte	Meals/ Drinks	Food Shop	Transport
9	Vizzavona	✓		✓	✓	✓	✓	🚌 🚆
10	Capannelle	✓	✓	✓	✓	✓	✓	
11a	Col de Verde	✓	✓	✓		✓	✓	
11b	Refuge de Prati	✓	✓	✓		✓	✓	
12	Refuge d'Usciolu	✓	✓	✓		✓	✓	
13a	Bergeries de Basseta	✓		✓		✓	✓	
13b	Refuge de Matalza	✓	✓	✓		✓	✓	
14a	Bergerie de Croci	✓	✓	✓		✓	✓	
14b	Refuge d'Asinau	✓	✓	✓		✓	✓	
15	Bavella Village	✓			✓	✓	✓	🚌
16a	Refuge d'I Paliri	✓	✓	✓		✓	✓	
16b	Conca	✓	✓	✓	✓	✓	✓	🚌

Food

Breakfast in Vizzavona: a rare treat on the GR20!

Corsican food is excellent but, other than the lovely cheeses and cured meats, you will not see much of it on the GR20. There are restaurants in Calenzana, Haut Asco, Vizzavona, Bavella and Conca but elsewhere, you will be far away from 'haute cuisine'. Generally, you will have the following food options:

Prepared meals at refuges/bergeries: cooked evening meals are available to everyone, whether camping or staying in refuge dormitories/fixed tents. They are simple (often pasta or rice) but expensive: the food has to be carried up from the valleys below or transported by helicopter. The quality varies but is often not particularly high: do not expect the excellent food that is found in refuges in the Alps. Make sure that you tell the manager (or gardien) on arrival if you would like breakfast and/or an evening meal and whether you have any dietary requirements. Vegetarians are normally catered for but it will be harder for vegans. Breakfast at refuges/bergeries is normally the functional minimum of coffee, bread and jam. Most refuges/bergeries also serve simple food at lunchtime (omelettes, soup or local cheeses/cold meats).

Buying supplies at refuges/bergeries: all refuges and many bergeries sell basic groceries (normally dried foods such as pasta/rice, canned foods and packet sauces). Lightweight freeze-dried meals are sometimes available too. Fresh fruit and vegetables are rarely on offer. You can cook or heat these foods using the communal gas cookers provided at refuges or bring your own camping stove. Food stocks vary from refuge to refuge and supplies tend to get depleted by the end of the season. You will have to take what you can get. The prices of groceries are relatively high because they have to be carried up from the valleys below or transported by helicopter: for example, a packet of pasta or rice costs around €5. Normally you will also be able to buy biscuits, cereal bars, dried fruit and nuts to keep you fuelled during the day.

Carrying food supplies from home: given the high prices and limited range of available foods on the GR20, many start the trek with stocks of food brought from home. However, food is heavy so unless you are travelling very quickly, you will not be able to start the trek with all the food you will require for the full distance. It is much better to accept at the outset that you can only carry a few days' food than to exhaust yourself in the early stages of the trek by carrying too much. If you are planning to carry some meals, stick to dried food: water is food's heaviest component. Freeze-dried meals for backpackers are excellent because they are light and are prepared simply by adding boiling water.

Getting to Corsica

Stage 1 is a long, hot climb

By air: there are four airports on Corsica: Ajaccio, Bastia, Calvi and Figari (near Porto-Vecchio). International flights are available from the UK and other parts of Europe. Alternatively, Air Corsica and Air France fly regularly from a variety of cities in mainland France. Travellers from outside Europe could fly to mainland Europe and then transfer to one of the flights to Corsica.

Calvi Airport is closest to the N end of the GR20 and Figari Airport is closest to Conca in the S. For those travelling to Corsica with no surplus baggage (other than what they will carry on the trek), perhaps the best solution is to fly into Calvi and out of Figari or vice versa. Flying into Calvi and out of Bastia (or vice versa) is also a good option. However, those who wish to store surplus baggage (see 'On the Trail') will probably prefer to fly in and out of the same town: Bastia is therefore a good choice as it is roughly halfway (in terms of travel time) between the start and finish of the trek.

By ferry: there are regular ferries to Corsica from Marseille, Nice and Toulon in France and Savona, Genoa and Livorno in Italy. On Corsica there are ports in Ajaccio, Bastia, Île Rousse, Porto-Vecchio and Propriano. At the date of press, the available ferries are summarised below.

Ferry Company	Mainland Port	Corsican Port
Corsica Ferries www.corsica-ferries.co.uk	France: Toulon, Nice Italy: Savona, Livorno, Piombino	Ajaccio, Bastia, Île Rousse, Porto-Vecchio
Corsica Linea www.corsicalinea.com	Marseille	Ajaccio, Bastia, Île Rousse, Propriano
La Méridionale www.lameridionale.fr	Marseille	Porto-Vecchio, Ajaccio
Moby Lines www.mobylines.com	Genoa, Livorno, Piombino	Bastia, Ajaccio

Travel to/from Trail-heads

Following the red/white flashes becomes second nature

Details for travel to and from the three main trail-heads (Calenzana, Vizzavona and Conca) are provided below. Buses are run by a variety of operators. For contact details for the specific bus companies, see 'Further Information' below. You can find general information on the available services at www.corsicabus.org, which is an unofficial website.

There are also a number of secondary escape/access points: see 'On the Trail'. Details for travel to and from these places are set out in the relevant route descriptions.

Crossing between the two boccas on Stage 3

Getting to Calenzana (N trail-head)

From	Travel to Calenzana
Calvi	**Taxi**: there are usually plenty of taxis in town and at the airport (20-30min; €40-45). If flying to Calvi, you can often find other people on the plane to share a taxi with. **Bus**: from the end of June to the start of September, les Beaux Voyages run twice each day from Calvi to Calenzana (and the opposite direction) (30min; €8). Outside of this period, the bus runs from Calvi to Calenzana (but not from Calenzana to Calvi) on school days only. **Walking**: Calvi is approximately 13km from Calenzana. Some walk along the roads or try to hitch-hike. The bus station in Calvi is a short walk from the port. Calvi airport is 7km S of Calvi: to travel into Calvi, take a taxi.
Île Rousse	**Taxi**: this is an expensive option if travelling alone but can be cost-effective for groups. It could save you a lot of time. From the port to Calenzana, it is approximately 28km (45min). **Train:** there are trains throughout the day from Île Rousse to Calvi (40min). For travel from Calvi to Calenzana, see above. **Bus**: in July/August, les Beaux Voyages run once or twice each day between Île Rousse and Calvi (30min). Outside this period, the service only runs on school days. For travel from Calvi to Calenzana, see above. The train station in Île Rousse is a short walk S from the ferry terminal. The Beaux Voyages bus stop is a 10min walk S of the train station.
Bastia	**Bus**: in July/August, les Beaux Voyages run once or twice each day between Bastia and Calvi (2hr). Outside this period, the service only runs on school days. For travel from Calvi to Calenzana, see above. **Train**: there are a few trains each day from Bastia to Calvi (3hr). For travel from Calvi to Calenzana, see above. The bus and train stations in Bastia are walking distance (W) from the ferry terminal. Bastia airport is 20km S of Bastia: to travel into Bastia, take a taxi (€50-65) or catch a bus (operated by Autobus Bastiais; 25min; €9).
Ajaccio	**Train**: there are a few trains each day from Ajaccio to Calvi (4.5hr). For travel from Calvi to Calenzana, see above. The train station in Ajaccio is a short walk N from the ferry terminal. Ajaccio airport is 6km from the train station: to travel into Ajaccio, take a taxi or catch bus no.8 which departs hourly (20-30min).
Porto-Vecchio	**Bus**: from mid-June to mid-September, Rapides Bleus run twice each day from Porto-Vecchio to Bastia. In July/August, this bus also stops at Bastia Airport. For travel from Bastia to Calvi and Calenzana, see above. The bus station in Porto-Vecchio is 1km NW of the ferry terminal: walk along the quay.
Figari	Transports Rossi runs a shuttle service from Figari Airport to Porto-Vecchio (30min). Alternatively, take a taxi (25min; €50-80). For travel from Porto-Vecchio to Calvi and Calenzana, see above.

Getting to Conca (S trail-head)

From	Travel to Conca
Porto-Vecchio	Rapides Bleus run two buses each day from Porto-Vecchio to Bastia, stopping at Ste Lucie de Porto-Vecchio (20-30min from Porto-Vecchio). From Ste Lucie de Porto-Vecchio, take a shuttle bus to Conca: these are timed to connect with the Rapides Bleus buses and are arranged with Gîte la Tonnelle in Conca (€4). Gîte la Tonnelle also runs a few shuttles each day directly from Porto-Vecchio to Conca. Alternatively, in July/August, Autocars Bradesi runs three shuttles each day from Porto-Vecchio to Conca (40min; €6.50). It is prudent to book buses and shuttles in advance. The bus station in Porto-Vecchio is 1km NW of the ferry terminal: walk along the quay.
Figari	Transports Rossi runs a shuttle service from Figari Airport to Porto-Vecchio (30min). Alternatively, take a taxi (25min; €50-80). For travel from Porto-Vecchio to Conca, see above.
Ajaccio	In July/August, Corsica Europa Travel runs three buses each day from Ajaccio to Porto-Vecchio (3.5hr; €20). Outside this period, the service is twice daily from Monday to Saturday but does not run on Sundays. For travel from Porto-Vecchio to Conca, see above. The bus station in Ajaccio is at the ferry terminal. Ajaccio airport is 6km from the centre: to travel into Ajaccio, take a taxi or catch bus no.8 which departs hourly (20-30min).
Bastia	Rapides Bleus runs two buses each day between Bastia and Porto-Vecchio, via Ste Lucie de Porto-Vecchio (20-30min from Porto-Vecchio). In July/August, this bus also stops at Bastia Airport. For travel from Ste Lucie de Porto-Vecchio to Conca, see above. The bus and train stations in Bastia are walking distance (W) from the ferry terminal. Bastia airport is 20km S of Bastia: to travel into Bastia, take a taxi (€50-65) or catch a bus (Autobus Bastiais; 25min; €9).
Île Rousse	**Train**: there are a few trains each day from Île Rousse to Bastia (2.5hr). For travel from Bastia to Conca, see above. **Bus**: in July/August, les Beaux Voyages runs once or twice each day between Bastia and Île Rousse (1.5hr). Outside this period, the service only runs on school days. For travel from Bastia to Conca, see above. The train station in Île Rousse is a short walk S from the ferry terminal. The Beaux Voyages bus stop is a 10min walk S of the train station.
Calvi	**Train**: there are a few trains each day from Calvi to Bastia (3hr). For travel from Bastia to Conca, see above. **Bus** : in July/August, les Beaux Voyages runs once or twice each day between Bastia and Calvi (2hr). Outside this period, the service only runs on school days. For travel from Bastia to Conca, see above. The train station in Calvi is a short walk from the port. The bus stop in Calvi is near the train station. Calvi airport is 7km S of Calvi: to travel into Calvi, take a taxi.

Getting to Vizzavona (middle trail-head)

From	Travel to Vizzavona
Bastia	There are trains throughout the day from Bastia to Ajaccio which all stop at Vizzavona (2.5-3hr). The train station in Bastia is walking distance (W) from the ferry terminal. Bastia airport is 20km S of Bastia: to travel into Bastia, take a taxi (€50-65) or catch a bus (Autobus Bastiais; 25min; €9).
Ajaccio	There are trains throughout the day from Ajaccio to Bastia which all stop at Vizzavona (1hr). The train station in Ajaccio is a short walk N from the ferry terminal. Ajaccio airport is 6km from the train station: to travel into Ajaccio, take a taxi or catch bus no.8 which departs hourly (20-30min).
Calvi	There are a few trains each day from Calvi to Ajaccio which all stop at Vizzavona (3.5hr). The train station in Calvi is a short walk from the port. The bus stop in Calvi is near the train station. Calvi airport is 7km S of Calvi: to travel into Calvi, take a taxi.
Île Rousse	There are a few trains each day from Île Rousse to Ajaccio which all stop at Vizzavona (3hr). The train station in Île Rousse is a short walk S of the ferry terminal.
Porto-Vecchio	This is a long transfer: get the bus to Bastia or Ajaccio and then transfer to the train to Vizzavona. Rapides Bleus runs buses twice a day between Porto-Vecchio and Bastia. In July/August, Corsica Europa Travel runs three times each day between Porto-Vecchio and Ajaccio (3.5hr; €20). Outside this period, the service is twice daily from Monday to Saturday but does not run on Sundays. For travel from Bastia and Ajaccio to Vizzavona, see above. The bus station in Porto-Vecchio is 1km NW of the ferry terminal: walk along the quay.
Figari	This is a long transfer: get the bus to Ajaccio and then transfer to the train to Vizzavona. In July/August, Corsica Europa Travel runs three buses each day between Porto-Vecchio and Ajaccio which stop at Figari village (3hr to Ajaccio; €20). Outside this period, the service is twice daily from Monday to Saturday but does not run on Sundays. For travel from Ajaccio to Vizzavona, see above. Figari village is 5km by taxi from Figari airport.

Getting away from Calenzana (N trail-head)

To	Travel from Calenzana
Calvi	**Taxi**: the businesses in Calenzana should be able to call a taxi for you or at least give you an up to date number for a taxi. A taxi to Calvi or Calvi Airport will take 20-30min (€40-45). **Bus**: from the end of June to the start of September, les Beaux Voyages run twice each day from Calenzana to Calvi (30min; €8). Outside of this period, there is no bus from Calenzana to Calvi. **Walking**: Calvi is approximately 13km from Calenzana. Some walk along the roads or try to hitch-hike. The bus and train stations in Calvi are a short walk from the port. Calvi airport is 7km S of Calvi by taxi.
Île Rousse	First travel to Calvi (see above). From there, trains leave throughout the day to Île Rousse (40min). Alternatively, in July/August, les Beaux Voyages runs one or two buses each day between Calvi and Île Rousse (30min). Outside this period, the service only runs on school days. You could also take a taxi from Calenzana to Île Rousse: an expensive option if travelling alone but can be cost-effective for groups. The businesses in Calenzana should be able to call a taxi for you or at least give you an up to date number for a taxi. Calenzana to Île Rousse is approximately 28km (45min). The train station in Île Rousse is a 10min walk N of the Beaux Voyages bus stop. The ferry terminal is a short walk N from the train station.
Bastia	First travel to Calvi (see above). From there, a few trains travel each day to Bastia (3hr). Alternatively, in July/August, les Beaux Voyages runs one or two buses each day from Calvi to Bastia (2hr). Outside this period, the service only runs on school days. The bus and train stations in Bastia are walking distance (W) from the ferry terminal. Bastia airport is 20km S of Bastia: to travel to the airport, take a taxi (€50-65) or catch a bus (Autobus Bastiais; 25min; €9).
Ajaccio	First travel to Calvi (see above). From Calvi, there are a few trains each day to Ajaccio (4.5hr). The train station in Ajaccio is a short walk N of the ferry terminal. Ajaccio airport is 6km from the train station: take a taxi or catch bus no.8 which departs hourly (20-30min).
Porto-Vecchio	First travel to Bastia (see above). From Bastia, Rapides Bleus runs two buses each day to Porto-Vecchio (mid-June to mid-September). The bus station in Porto-Vecchio is 1km NW of the ferry terminal: walk along the quay.
Figari	First travel to Porto-Vecchio (see above). From Porto Vecchio, Transports Rossi runs a shuttle service to Figari Airport (30min). Alternatively take a taxi (25min; €50-80).

Getting away from Conca (S trail-head)

To	Travel from Conca
Porto-Vecchio	Gîte la Tonnelle runs shuttles throughout the day directly from Conca to Porto-Vecchio: the schedule is irregular as they depart when full. Alternatively, in July/August, Autocars Bradesi runs three shuttles each day from Conca to Porto-Vecchio (40min; €6.50). It is prudent to book shuttles in advance. The bus station in Porto-Vecchio is 1km NW of the ferry terminal: walk along the quay.
Figari	First travel to Porto-Vecchio (see above). From there, Transports Rossi runs shuttles to Figari Airport (30min). Alternatively take a taxi from Porto-Vecchio to Figari Airport (25min; €50-80).
Ajaccio	First travel to Porto-Vecchio (see above). In July/August, Corsica Europa Travel runs three buses each day from Porto-Vecchio to Ajaccio (3.5hr; €20). Outside this period, the service is twice daily from Monday to Saturday but does not run on Sundays. The bus station in Ajaccio is at the ferry terminal. Ajaccio airport is 6km from the train station: take a taxi or catch bus no.8 which departs hourly (20-30min).
Bastia	Gîte la Tonnelle runs shuttles from Conca to Ste Lucie de Porto-Vecchio (€4). Rapides Bleus runs twice a day to Bastia from Ste Lucie de Porto-Vecchio (2.5hr). In July/August, this bus also stops at Bastia Airport. The shuttles are timed to connect with the Rapides Bleus buses. The bus and train stations in Bastia are walking distance (W) from the ferry terminal. Bastia airport is 20km S of Bastia: take a taxi (€50-65) or catch a bus (Autobus Bastiais; 25min; €9).
Île Rousse	First travel to Bastia (see above). From there, a few trains travel each day to Île Rousse (2.5hr). Alternatively, in July/August, les Beaux Voyages runs one or two buses each day between Bastia and Île Rousse (1.5hr). Outside this period, the service only runs on school days. The train station in Île Rousse is a 10min walk N of the Beaux Voyages bus stop. The ferry terminal is a short walk N from the train station.
Calvi	First travel to Bastia (see above). From there, a few trains travel each day to Calvi (3hr). Alternatively, in July/August, les Beaux Voyages runs one or two buses each day between Bastia and Calvi (2hr). Outside this period, the service only runs on school days. The train station in Calvi is a short walk from the port. The bus stop in Calvi is near the train station. Calvi airport is 7km S of Calvi: take a taxi.

Getting away from Vizzavona (middle trail-head)

To	Travel from Vizzavona
Bastia	There are daily trains to Bastia (2.5-3hr). The bus and train stations in Bastia are walking distance (W) from the ferry terminal. Bastia airport is 20km S of Bastia: take a taxi (€50-65) or catch a bus (Autobus Bastiais; 25min; €9).
Ajaccio	There are daily trains to Ajaccio (1hr). The train station in Ajaccio is a short walk N of the ferry terminal. Ajaccio airport is 6km from the train station: take a taxi or catch bus no.8 which departs hourly (20-30min).
Calvi	There are daily trains to Calvi (3.5hr). The train station in Calvi is a short walk from the port. The bus stop in Calvi is near the train station. Calvi airport is 7km S of Calvi by taxi.
Île Rousse	There are daily trains to Île Rousse (3hr). The ferry terminal is a short walk N from the train station.
Porto-Vecchio	This is a long transfer: take the train from Vizzavona to Bastia or Ajaccio (see above) and then catch a bus to Porto-Vecchio. Rapides Bleus runs buses twice a day between Bastia and Porto-Vecchio. In July/August, Corsica Europa Travel runs three buses each day between Ajaccio and Porto-Vecchio (3.5hr; €20). Outside this period, the service is twice daily from Monday to Saturday but does not run on Sundays. The bus station in Porto-Vecchio is 1km NW of the ferry terminal: walk along the quay.
Figari	This is a long transfer: take the train to Ajaccio and then catch a bus to Figari village. In July/August, Corsica Europa Travel runs three buses each day between Ajaccio and Porto-Vecchio which stop at Figari village (3hr from Ajaccio; €20). Outside this period, the service is twice daily from Monday to Saturday but does not run on Sundays. Figari airport is 5km by taxi from Figari village.

Further information:

Shuttles: **Gîte la Tonnelle** in Conca (+33 (0)4 95 71 46 55; latonnelleconca@hotmail.com); **Autocars Bradesi** (+33 (0)4 95 71 40 09); **Transports Rossi** (+33 (0)4 95 71 00 11)

Trains: **Chemins de Fer de la Corse** (www.cf-corse.corsica)

Buses: **les Beaux Voyages** (www.corsicar.com; +33 (0)4 95 65 11 35); **Autobus Bastiais** (+33 (0)4 95 31 06 65); **Rapides Bleus** (www.rapides-bleus.com; +33 (0)4 95 72 35 57/(0)4 95 31 03 79); **Corsica Europa Travel** (+33 (0)4 95 71 24 64); **Ajaccio Airport Bus** (mobilite.muvitarra.fr)

Taxis: contact details for taxis constantly change so ask locally or search the internet

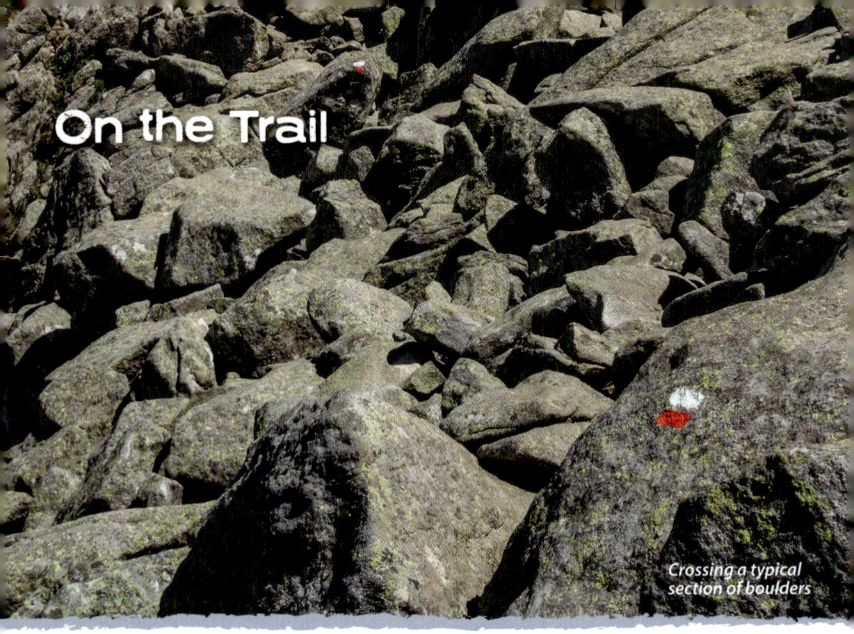

Crossing a typical section of boulders

Costs

As vacations go, long-distance walking in Europe is relatively inexpensive. The walking itself is free as no permits are required. For most trekkers, a large proportion of daily expenditure will be on food and accommodation/camping at refuges: approximate costs are set out below. Costs at private bergeries may be a little higher. The few gîtes and hotels along the route are a lot more expensive.

	Approximate Cost (subject to change)
Dormitory bed in refuge (booked in advance)	€17
Fixed tent at refuge (booked in advance)	€13 for the tent rental (in total) + €9 per person
Camping at refuge with trekker's own tent (booked in advance)	€9 per person
Breakfast at refuge	€8-10
Evening meal at refuge	€16-22
Beer (0.5 litre)	€6-7
Cola	€3-4

Weather

Mountains can be dangerous so treat them with respect and caution, even if the weather forecast is favourable. The GR20 travels through high mountain terrain: many of the Corsican summits are over 2000m. The weather in the trekking season is normally very hot and sunny, even at altitude. Accordingly, it is prudent to start walking very early in the morning to take advantage of the coolest part of the day: some trekkers rise as early as 05:00 or 06:00.

However, conditions can change quickly so you should also be prepared for rain. Furthermore, the Corsican mountains are notorious for their afternoon thunderstorms. In the mornings, the blazing Mediterranean sun heats up the mountains and, as the day progresses, cooler air is drawn in from the sea: clouds therefore build throughout the day, often culminating in rain and fearsome thunderstorms in the afternoon. Thunderstorms are most common in July and August. High altitude sections of the GR20 can be dangerous during thunderstorms and on rare occasions, trekkers are killed by lightning. Start walking very early in the morning so that you have finished for the day by the time thunderstorms arrive.

The suspension bridge on Stage 3

The region has a number of micro-climates with the weather often differing from valley to valley. It is possible therefore to find blazing sunshine on one side of a pass and cloud or rain over the other side.

Snow covers the mountains in winter: high passes can remain snow-covered until mid-June, making short sections of the GR20 difficult and/or dangerous. In such conditions, crampons and/or an ice-axe might be helpful. Snow can also fall on mountain passes and summits during the summer, although this is rare. You may find information on current snow conditions on the Instagram page of the Corsica Mountain Rescue Team (@equipemontagnepnrc) or the PNRC Facebook page (@ParcNaturelRegionalCorse). Our GR20 Facebook group also usually has updates: see **www.facebook.com/groups/CorsicaGR20**.

Météo-France, the French meteorological office, provides national, regional and local forecasts at www.meteofrance.com. It also has an excellent smartphone app which provides, free of charge, regularly updated local forecasts. Many other internet sites and apps also provide forecasts, with a varying degree of reliability. Alternatively, ask the refuge managers whose local knowledge of weather is often invaluable: follow their advice if they tell you it is not safe to set out.

Maps

In this book, we have included the best maps available. Each sub-stage has its own 1:25,000 scale map produced by IGN, the French mapping agency. Occasionally, a map has been reduced slightly to fit on the page. Although these maps are normally sufficient for navigation, a sheet map can be helpful, particularly in bad weather. Also, with a sheet map you get a better feel for the geography of the region as it helps you to identify peaks and landmarks sighted along the way.

Four IGN 1:25,000 sheets are required to cover the whole trek: 4250OT Corte/Monte Cinto, 4251OT Monte-d'Oro/Monte-Rotondo, 4252OT Monte-Renoso/Bastelica and 4253ET Aiguilles de Bavella/Solenzara. IGN has also produced a 1:50,000 map, Traversée de la Corse GR20, which shows the whole route on one sheet. Alternatively, Libris/Éditions Didier Richard produce an excellent 1:50,000 map: it folds down very small and shows the whole GR20.

However, perhaps the best overall solution is to combine the real maps provided in this book with IGN's excellent smartphone app: it provides 1:25,000 maps for the whole of France for around £20/$30. The app uses GPS to show your location and direction on the map.

Paths and waymarking

On the GR20, you will need to take great care at all times. The rocky terrain is very challenging, particularly on the N half of the route. Large sections of the trek have no path and frequently, you must cross long sections of boulders. For this reason, the route has been extremely well marked. In fact, it is possibly the best-waymarked trail in the world: most of the red/white markings have been carefully placed to be in the line of sight of the previous one. You are rarely out of eye-shot of a waymark: if, at any time, you find that you cannot see one then you have probably gone wrong and should backtrack to the previous waymark. In good conditions therefore navigation is usually straightforward. You quickly get into a rhythm, looking for the next waymark every time you pass one. In the route descriptions, we do not highlight every junction because the waymarking is so good: generally we only mention junctions if they are particularly significant or if there are no waymarks.

A typical waymark

Given the effectiveness of the waymarks, signposts are rare. Bear in mind though that waymarking is at the mercy of the environment: markings can fade or be obscured by rockfalls or landslides.

When there is a path, it is often rocky and tiring to walk on (particularly in the N sections). Paths improve on the S half of the route but there are still some difficult parts. There is much scrambling (particularly on the N half) and you will frequently need to use your hands. Sometimes cables or railings have been bolted into the rocks to assist you on particularly difficult or exposed sections. The difficulties are exacerbated by the fact that you will probably be carrying a heavier pack than usual. Fortunately, the granite rocks provide good grip in dry conditions but they are more slippery in the wet: take even greater care if it has rained.

In summary, walking the GR20 requires almost continuous concentration. On the challenging terrain, the chances of a fall are greater than usual and if you fall then the chance of injury on the rocky surfaces is high. You will spend more time than normal looking at where you put your feet. And you will use muscles that you did not know that you had. It is physically and mentally exhausting.

Some of the most challenging sections of the GR20 are listed below.

- **Stage 2:** challenging throughout with large sections of rocks and boulders on both climbs and descents. Watch your footing on the unstable surfaces. This stage is best avoided if you have a fear of heights.
- **Stage 3:** there is a tough climb across rock slabs with cables to assist. Finish with a knee-jerking descent.
- **Stage 4:** the climb is very long and exposed and you will have to scramble up boulders and slabs: there are cables to assist. Approaching Pointe des Éboulis, you climb a steep and unstable slope: leave a large gap between yourself and any person above to avoid injury from rock-falls. This stage is best avoided if you have a fear of heights.
- **Stage 7:** possibly the hardest stage of the GR20. There is another long, steep climb with boulders and slabs to scramble over. Approaching Bocca alle Porte, you climb a steep and unstable slope: leave a large gap between yourself and any person above to avoid injury from rock-falls. Afterwards, you must descend some vertical sections of rocks with cables to assist: a fall would have serious consequences. After another steep climb (with some scrambling), there is a knee-jerking descent to the refuge. This stage is best avoided if you have a fear of heights.
- **Stage 12:** an undulating stage which is very tiring. There are sections of scrambling and boulders to cross.
- **Stage 14b:** the final descent to Refuge d'Asinau is extremely steep and exposed in places. Some scrambling is required: take great care.

Water

Even more so than on other treks, drinking water should be one of your primary considerations each day. The sun in Corsica is extremely hot. Dehydration and sunstroke are possibilities so you will probably need more water than usual: perhaps three to five litres per day. However, water is heavy so it is preferable not to start the day carrying such large quantities. You should therefore plan carefully so that you know where your next fill-up point will be. There is normally a source of drinking water at refuges and private bergeries. Depending on the season, water is also available from rivers and streams: generally water-courses are fullest in June and decline throughout the walking season.

The source at Refuge d'I Paliri

We list the main water sources in the introduction to each stage but we have not included all streams and rivers as the availability of water there varies according to season. It is good practice to fill your water bottles each day before leaving the refuge/bergerie. Start with at least two litres per person. Furthermore, always check your water levels when you pass a source. It is unwise to rely completely on the availability of water in rivers and streams: they might be dry when you arrive.

Most people drink from the sources at refuges/bergeries without treating or filtering the water. Many walkers also drink untreated water from rivers/streams without any issues. However, others insist upon filtering or treating water to minimise the risk of contaminants. You will have to weigh up the risks and make up your own mind. If, like many, you do decide to drink the water untreated, there are a few rules that you should follow to reduce any risk:

- Avoid water where there is evidence nearby of animals, especially cows or sheep: carcasses (of dead animals) or faeces can cause contamination
- Do not collect water downstream from buildings or grazing areas
- Only drink from moving water. The faster the better
- The bigger the river/stream the better
- Generally the higher the altitude the better

If you do wish to treat your water, this can be done by way of portable filters, steripens or purification chemicals. The effectiveness of the different products and methods varies and is beyond the scope of this book so do your research before your trip.

Escape/access points

As well as the main trail-heads at Calenzana, Vizzavona and Conca, the GR20 has some secondary escape/access points, enabling a walker to join or leave the route. However, the availability of public transport at these locations varies by season. The key escape/access points are listed below: full details (including transport options) are set out in the relevant route descriptions.

- Haut Asco (Stage 3)
- Albertacce (off-route from Stage 5a)
- Castel de Vergio (Stage 5c)
- Cristinacce (off-route from Stage 6a)
- Bergerie de Grottelle (off-route from Stage 7)
- Tattone (off-route from Stage 8)
- Cozzano (off-route from Stage 13a)
- Zicavo (off-route from Stages 13a and 13b)
- Bavella (Stage 15)

Storing bags

Often walkers from Europe travel to Corsica carrying only the gear that they will actually take on the trek. However, trekkers from further afield, and those who want to spend some time on Corsica after the trek, will probably have additional baggage which they need to store while trekking. Normally a hotel that you have stayed in will let you store bags until your return: check when booking. However, you will want to leave your bag in a location which is straightforward to return to at the end of the trek. Whichever direction you decide to trek, if you leave bags close to your start point then you will have a long journey at the end to get back to them. For that reason, many choose to arrive on Corsica at Bastia and leave from the same point, storing their baggage in the hotel in Bastia that they stay in.

Gas canisters

Gas canisters for camping stoves are available along the route at refuges and shops. Both screw-in and Campinggaz canisters can be found but stocks of each vary and occasionally, run out. Airlines will not allow you to transport gas so, unless you arrive on Corsica by ferry, you will want to source gas on arrival before setting out on the trek.

If trekking N-S, the Spar shop in Calenzana stocks both types of canister: if you speak French, it is wise to call before travelling to Calenzana and check if they have them in stock (+33 (0)4 95 62 73 95). Alternatively, you can buy them in shops in Calvi including Super U and Intersport.

If trekking S-N, you may be able to get gas at Gîte la Tonnelle in Conca. Alternatively, shops in Ajaccio, Porto-Vecchio and Bastia sell canisters, including Intersport. In Vizzavona, the halfway point of the trek, canisters are available in the shops and at the campsite.

If you fail to obtain one before starting, then you can still use the communal gas cookers at the refuges until you are able to buy a canister. Furthermore, it is not uncommon to find half-used canisters left behind at the refuge cooking areas near the ends of the route: trekkers off-load surplus gas to save weight, knowing that other trekkers who are starting out will pick them up.

Waymarking on Stage 12

Equipment

The Golo Valley (Stage 5c)

If you have read this far, then you will be aware that the GR20 is hard. It is made harder still by the need to carry more than on many other European treks. Even if you stay in refuges or fixed tents, you will still need to carry a sleeping bag which in turn requires you to carry a larger (and comparatively heavier) backpack. And because the refuges on the GR20 are small and book up quickly, most trekkers carry their own camping equipment. On a normal trek it is difficult enough to carry camping gear but on the GR20, the burden of the extra weight is magnified by the challenges of the terrain and the climate.

Furthermore, the wide range of possible weather conditions in the Corsican mountains impacts the weight of your pack too. When undertaking any long-distance route, you should be properly equipped for the worst terrain and the worst weather conditions which you could encounter: in Corsica that means the full range of sun, heat, rain, cold and possibly snow. You must carry clothing to combat all of these conditions. Although sun and heat will be your most common adversaries, being cold and wet at high altitude is unpleasant and can be dangerous.

However, the dilemma is that you should also consider weight and avoid carrying anything unnecessary. The heavier your pack, the harder the climbs will be. It is fair to say that most trekkers set off carrying equipment which is unnecessary or simply too heavy: this often results in injury and/or exhaustion, leading to abandonment. You have complete control over what you bring and so you should give equipment choice careful consideration.

A trekkers base weight is the weight of his/her pack, excluding food and water. If you are not carrying your own tent and cooking equipment, it is perfectly possible to get by with a base weight of 6kg (13lb) or less. If you intend to carry camping equipment then, by investing in some modern lightweight gear, you could start the trek with a base weight of 8kg (17lb) or less. Many people are quick to tell you that the lighter the gear, the greater the price but that is not always the case. While it is true that lightweight gear can be expensive, there are also some excellent lightweight products which are great value. Tents, sleeping bags and backpacks are the three heaviest items that you will carry so they offer the biggest opportunities for weight-saving. But do not ignore the smaller items either as the weight can quickly add up.

Pack weight is so important on the GR20 that, if you can afford it, it is sensible to invest some money in gear before you go. The lighter your gear, the more you will enjoy the trek and the better your chance of success. Be ruthless as every ounce counts.

Recommended basic kit

Layering of clothing is the key to warmth. Do not wear cotton: it does not dry quickly and gets cold. Modern walking clothes are light so make sure that you have a spare set to change into if you get wet.

Boots/Shoes	Good quality, properly fitting and worn in. Some hike in trail-running shoes but others prefer boots with ankle support. The granite rock on the GR20 is notoriously hard on footwear so ensure that your soles are tough. Ventilation is important too and the all-leather boots commonly used in the UK will probably be too hot.
Socks	3 pairs of good quality, quick-drying walking socks: wash one, wear one, spare one. Wash them regularly and change them daily, helping to avoid blisters.
Camp shoes	Such as flip-flops or crocs. If you have comfortable boots then you might consider not bringing any to save weight.
Waterproof jacket and trousers	A waterproof and breathable rain jacket is essential although it might never leave your pack. Most people do not bother with waterproof trousers on the GR20 but if you are unlucky with the weather then you might be glad of them.
Base layers	3 T-shirts and pants of man-made fabrics or merino wool, which wick moisture away from your body: wash one, wear one, spare one.
Fleeces	2 fleeces. Man-made fabrics.
Shorts/ Trousers	2 pairs of shorts or walking trousers. Convertible trousers are practical as you can remove the legs on warm days. One pair of shorts and one pair of trousers is also a good choice.
Gloves	Early or late season trekkers may wish to bring gloves.
Warm hat	Always carry a warm hat. Even in summer it can be cold at altitude, especially in the evening and early morning.
Down jacket	You may not use it but even in summer it can be cold at altitude. In early and late season, low temperatures are more likely, especially in the evening and early morning.
Sunglasses, sun hat, sunscreen and lip salve	The sun in Corsica is brutal and relentless so do not set out without these items.
Sleeping bag	Refuges do not provide bedding. See below for information on sleeping bags.
Head-light with spare batteries	You will need a flashlight in both refuges and tents. Furthermore, it is good practice to carry one for emergencies: it can assist if you get caught out late and enable you to signal to rescuers.

Backpack	The weight of a backpack itself is often overlooked but it can be the single heaviest thing that you will carry. The difference in the weights of various packs can be surprisingly large: get a light one. 35-40 litres should be sufficient unless you are carrying camping gear. If you are carrying camping gear, then 45-60 litres should be sufficient. If you need a pack bigger than these then you are most likely carrying too much. Look for well-padded shoulder straps and waist band. Much of the weight of the pack should sit on your hips rather than your shoulders. If your budget extends to it, we highly recommend the packs made by the US manufacturer Zpacks: they are a fraction of the weight of most other packs. The Zpacks Arc Blast is 55 litres yet it weighs just over 500g (20 oz).
Waterproof pack-liner	Most backpacks are not very waterproof. A liner will keep your gear dry if it rains.
Whistle	For emergencies. Many rucksacks have one incorporated into the sternum strap.
Basic first-aid kit	Including plasters, a bandage, antiseptic wipes and painkillers. Blister plasters, moleskin padding or tape (such as Leukotape) can be useful to prevent or combat blisters.
Map and compass	For maps see above. A GPS unit or a smartphone app can be a useful addition but they are no substitute for a map and compass: after all, batteries can run out and electronics can fail.
Knife	Such as a Swiss Army knife. You are going to need to cut that cheese!
Walking poles	These transfer weight from your legs onto your arms, keeping you fresher. They also save your knees (particularly on descents) and can reduce the likelihood of falling or twisting an ankle.
Phone and charger (with EU adapter)	A smartphone is a very useful tool on a trek. It can be used for emergencies. Furthermore, apps for weather, mapping and hotel booking are invaluable. It can also replace your camera to save weight.
Portable charger	Some refuges facilitate the charging of electronic devices but you will pay for it and you will probably have to queue. However, in most places, there will be nowhere to charge up. It is therefore a good idea to buy a battery pack: Anker make some excellent ones.
Toiletries	**Shower gel**: a small hotel-size bottle should be enough to last the trek, saving a lot of weight. **Toothbrush and toothpaste**: an almost empty tube will save weight. For those who shave, **shaving oil** is a lightweight alternative to a can of foam. Leave that make-up behind!
Towel	Lightweight trekking towel. Refuges do not provide towels.

Toilet paper and trowel	Refuges do not provide toilet paper, however, they do sell it. Bring a backpacking trowel in case nature calls on the trail: bury toilet waste and carry out used toilet paper. Leave no trace.
Ziplock plastic bag	A lightweight way of keeping money, passport and credit cards dry.
Ear plugs	Useful if staying in refuge dormitories: you will thank us if someone snores!
Crampons/ Ice-axe	If trekking at the start of June, some high passes may be covered with snow.
Water	Start each day with at least two litres of water per person. Hydration packs with tubes facilitate more effective hydration by enabling drinking on the move. Bring a filter or purification tablets if required.
Food	Carry some emergency food. Energy bars, nuts and dried fruit are all good.

Additional gear for campers

Tent: this is one of the heaviest things that you will carry so it provides a big opportunity for weight saving. Some 2-person tents weigh more than 3kg while others weigh less than 0.6kg. The heaviest ones are normally built for extreme winter conditions and are overkill for the Corsican summer. The lightest ones are quite fragile for the spiky and rocky Corsican ground unless you are very careful. Our advice is to aim for a tent weighing 1 to 1.5kg. Although a few premium brands charge a lot for their products and there are some very expensive tents at the lightest end of the scale, these days there are plenty of lightweight tents available at a reasonable price. Consider money spent here as an investment in your well-being and enjoyment of one of the world's great trails. Believe us when we say that a few kgs can be the difference between success and failure.

The Corsican ground is hard and rocky and it can be difficult to get pegs into it. Accordingly, free-standing tents (which can stand up on their own before being pegged) perform much better than those that need to be firmly pegged to stand upright. Furthermore, level pitches are hard to find on the GR20 so a free-standing tent allows you easily to move the tent once erected.

Your tent should be waterproof to ensure that you stay dry during rainy nights or afternoon thunderstorms. If you are going to use a very light tent then a footprint can be a good idea to protect the base of the tent against the sharp Corsican rocks: 'footprint' is a trendy modern word for what used to be known as a groundsheet. Sometimes you can buy footprints specific to your tent model but we prefer to use a sheet of Tyvek which can be cut to size: Tyvek is extremely tough and is cheaper, and normally lighter, than most branded footprints.

Tent pegs: tent weights provided by manufacturers normally exclude the weight of the pegs. The pegs actually provided with tents tend to be quite heavy and many trekkers buy replacement ones which are lighter. Six heavy pegs can weigh as much as 240g while 6 light pegs can weigh as little as 6g. There are many different types available these days and it is important to match the peg with the type of ground they will be used on. The Corsican ground is hard so you will need a strong peg: the very lightest pegs will not survive but there are some excellent titanium ones available which weigh 40-50g for six.

Sleeping bag: each bag has a 'comfort rating': this is the lowest temperature at which the standard woman should enjoy a comfortable night's sleep. There is also a 'lower comfort limit' which is for men. That may sound simple but it is not. Although all reputable sleeping bag manufacturers use the same independent standard, the bags are not tested in the same place so there is a lack of consistency amongst ratings. Also, the ratings are designed with an average man and woman in mind but every person is different: some people get colder than others. The ratings should therefore be used as a guide only and it is wise to choose a bag with a rating which is at least five degrees lower than the night temperatures that you will encounter. In late June, July and August a bag rated between 0 and 10°C is normally sufficient, depending on whether you 'sleep hot' or 'sleep cold'. In early and late season, you may want something warmer. However, you will not want to bring a bag that is much too warm as that would add unnecessary weight to your pack.

Unfortunately, with sleeping bags, price tends to be inversely proportional to weight. This is largely because the lightest bags are filled with goose/duck down which is expensive. Synthetic bags are also available but they are much heavier so down is the better choice for the GR20. The disadvantage of down bags is that they can lose their warmth if they get wet but that is less likely on the GR20 particularly if you have a good tent and pack-liner. Our advice is first to decide what comfort rating you will require. Then choose the lightest bag (with that rating) which you can afford.

Sleeping mat: this serves two purposes. Firstly, it makes it comfortable for you to sleep on the hard ground. Secondly, it insulates you from the ground's cold surface. There are three types: air, self-inflating and closed-cell foam. The advantages and disadvantages of each are set out below. For the GR20, weight is normally more of an issue than warmth so we prefer air mats.

Sleeping Mat Type	Pros	Cons
Air mats: need to be blown up	Lightest Very comfortable Most compact when packed Thicker: good for side sleepers	Most expensive Hard work to inflate Can be punctured Less warm than self-inflating
Self-inflating: a combination of air and closed-cell foam. The mat partially inflates itself when the valve is opened	Warmest Very comfortable Quite compact More durable than air mats Firmness is adjustable by adding air	Heavier More expensive than closed-cell foam Can be punctured
Closed-cell foam	Light Least expensive Most durable Cannot be punctured	Not compact: needs to be strapped to the outside of your pack Least warm Least comfortable

Pillow: some use rolled-up clothing but we prefer an inflatable trekking pillow: they weigh around 50g.

Stove: you should choose a stove that uses the type of fuel which is available on the GR20. Airlines do not permit you to carry fuel on planes so, if you are flying to Corsica, you will need to source fuel on arrival. Although 'alcool à bruler' (similar to methylated spirits) is sometimes available in towns, gas is the only reliably available fuel on the GR20 itself (see 'On the Trail'). Accordingly, almost everyone who carries a stove chooses one which burns gas.

The GR20 is notoriously hard on footwear

In France, Campinggaz stoves are the most popular and there are two types of Campinggaz canisters for backpacking: pierceable and twist-on. Both of these are widely available but the twist-on ones are more common on the GR20. However, most stoves these days are designed to fit generic screw-on canisters (not Campinggaz) and accordingly, most international backpackers carry such stoves. To meet this demand, screw-on canisters are now widely available on the GR20 and a stove that takes screw-on gas canisters is probably the best choice.

Hundreds of different stoves are available, some more complicated than others. Often the lightest ones are the most simple and often the most simple ones are relatively inexpensive. If, like most, you will eat dried food such as pasta and rice then your stove will need to do little more than boil water. A basic stove which mounts on top of a gas canister will therefore be adequate: such a stove should also be cheap and lightweight (less than 100g).

Pots: if, like most, you eat dried food such as pasta and rice then you will only need one pot which will do little more than boil water. To save weight, go for the smallest pot that you can get away with. For example, if you are travelling solo and planning to use freeze-dried backpacking meals then you would need nothing bigger than a 500-600ml pot. Titanium pots are usually the lightest but they are slightly more expensive. Get the lightest one that you can afford.

Fork/Spoon: we love Sporks! They are made of plastic and have a spoon at one end and a fork at the other. They weigh a mere 9g and cost very little.

Bocca di u Sordu (Stage 16b)

Safety

Lac de Nino (Stage 6a)

On a calm summer's day, the Corsican mountains are paradise. But a sudden weather shift or an injury can change things dramatically so treat the mountains with respect and be conscious of your experience levels and physical capabilities. The following is a non-exhaustive list of recommendations:

- On the GR20, you frequently need to use your hands to scramble up or down rocks, boulders and slabs. Do not scramble with walking poles in your hands. Stow them away before you start to scramble to keep your hands free. The number of trekkers you see on the GR20 clambering up exposed rocks with poles in their hands is staggering: this is very dangerous.
- When scrambling, take your time. Leave large gaps between yourself and the person in front. Wait for others in front to finish their climb before commencing yours: if they were to fall, they could injure you.
- Start early to avoid ascending during the hottest part of the day and to allow more surplus time in case something goes wrong. Starting early also makes it more likely that you will be safely in camp before any thunderstorms arrive.
- Follow the advice of the refuge managers. If they tell you that it is not safe to set out, then do not do so.
- Do not stray from the route so as to avoid getting lost and to help prevent erosion of the landscape.
- Avoid exposed high ground in a thunderstorm. If you get caught out in one then drop your walking poles and stay away from trees, overhanging rocks, metal structures and caves. Generally accepted advice is to squat on your pack and keep as low as possible.
- Before you set out each day, study the route and make plans based upon the abilities of the weakest member of your party.
- Get a weather forecast (daily if possible) and reassess your plans in light of it. Avoid exposed routes if the weather is uncertain.
- Never be too proud to turn back if you find the going too tough or if the weather deteriorates.
- Bring a map and compass and know how to use them.
- Carry surplus food and clothing for emergencies.
- In the event of an accident, move an injured person into a safe place and administer any necessary first-aid. Keep the victim warm. Establish your exact coordinates and, if possible, use your cell-phone to call for help. The emergency number is set out on page 1. If you have no signal then send someone for help.
- When cooking, place your stove on the ground. Do not use it on a picnic table. We witnessed a walker knocking over his stove and spilling boiling water on his legs: his GR20 was immediately over.
- The fitter you are at the start of your trip, the more you will enjoy the walking.

General Information

The barren terrain seen on Stage 4

Language: French is the main language. The old language of Corsican is also still spoken by some inhabitants. These days, many locals working in the huts will have some basic English at least. Corsica is in France and there are many French trekkers on the GR20: on the trail, it is therefore good manners to make an effort to say 'hello' in French.

Charging electronic devices: Continental 2-pin plugs are used so visitors from outside Continental Europe will need an adapter. Some refuges facilitate the charging of electronic devices but others do not. Many trekkers carry portable battery packs (see 'Recommended basic kit').

Money: France uses the Euro(€). Hotels will probably take credit cards but you will need cash for almost everything else. There are no ATMs on the route so make sure that you have enough cash (for the entire trek) before travelling to the trail-heads.

Visas: citizens of the European Union do not need a visa to visit France. At the time of writing, citizens of Australia, New Zealand, Canada and the US do not need a visa for stays of up to three months.

Cell-phones: cell-phone network along the GR20 is better than it used to be but cannot be relied upon. Sometimes, you might only get network on high parts of the trail such as mountain passes. When network is available, it is likely to be a 4G/5G service enabling access to the internet from smartphones.

International dialling codes: the country code for France is +33. If dialling from overseas, the '0' in French area codes is omitted.

Wifi: hotels and gîtes may have wifi but otherwise, there is none on the GR20.

Insurance: mountain rescue services may not be free and therefore it is wise to have adequate insurance which covers hiking. Visitors from the UK should also make sure that they have the free Global Health Insurance Card (GHIC) but remember that often this will only cover part of your medical treatment so insurance is still recommended. Also, the GHIC will not cover any rescue itself.

Emergencies: the emergency telephone number is 112.

Ticks/bed-bugs: as is often the case in Europe, ticks are present in Corsica. They can carry Lyme disease or tick-borne encephalitis so check yourself regularly. Remove ticks with tweezers (making sure that you get all of it out) and then disinfect the area. Bed-bugs are a persistent problem in Corsica, particularly in refuge dormitories/fixed tents where they quickly spread in trekkers' sleeping bags. Most bed-bugs do not spread disease but their bites are unpleasant. Their presence encourages many trekkers to endure the burden of carrying their own tents.

A mouflon seen on Stage 2

Wildlife

Early morning is the best time for seeing wildlife and the first party on the trail has the best chance of a sighting.

Mouflon: a wild species of long-horned mountain sheep present in the Asco Valley and the Cinto and Bavella mountain ranges. It is the emblem of Corsica and is a protected species. They are difficult to spot.

Wild boar: a member of the pig family with small tusks. They are common in forests but hard to spot. In the unlikely event that you see one, keep your distance because they can be dangerous.

Corsican pigs: semi-wild pigs ('porc nustrale') which are reared for food. They are allowed to roam freely and forage in the forests. They are often a mixture of wild boar and domestic pig and are easy to spot. They are known to raid trekkers' bags for food at night so in certain places (such as Col de Verde) make sure that you keep your food inside your tent.

Deer: they became extinct in Corsica in the 1960s. In the late 20th century, deer were reintroduced from the neighbouring island of Sardinia but they are still very rare.

Other mammals: foxes are common, particularly at lower altitudes. You will often see goats grazing in the mountains. Squirrels, badgers and mice are fairly common below the tree-line. There are also bats.

Fish: species of trout and freshwater eels are found in rivers, streams and lakes.

Birds: red kites, buzzards, peregrine falcons, kestrels, owls and sparrowhawks are all present in Corsica. There are also golden eagles but they are rare. Small numbers of Gypaète Barbu (or Bearded Vulture) remain in Corsica: this is a vulture with a wingspan of up to 3m. In German, it was named 'Lammergeier' ('lamb-hawk') because it was believed that it attacked lambs.

Reptiles and amphibians: lizards are very common. Harder to spot are the salamanders which are slow-moving, black and yellow amphibians: you may see them crossing paths in woods (see page 132). There are also grass snakes and land tortoises (which have almost disappeared from other parts of France).

Plants and Flowers

On Corsica flowers can thrive in the most unlikely places

Corsica is famous for its 'maquis', a carpet of aromatic (and often spiky) Mediterranean vegetation. However, as it rarely grows above 600m, you will see little of it on the GR20. However, in the Corsican mountains, you will see plenty of other plants. Trees in the mountains include silver fir, oak, hornbeam, beech, chestnut and the endemic Corsican pine. There are also plenty of shrubs, many of which are prickly (such as broom with its yellow flowers and juniper). One of the most common plants are alder bushes: you will often see them beside the trail but their lovely scent is more remarkable than their appearance.

Corsica is also home to hundreds of wild-flowers, many of which are endemic. They can grow in the most unlikely of places, even in the middle of dry, rocky terrain. June is a fabulous month for flowers. At this time, carpets of different colours cover the lower slopes and pastures. Although spring is the peak time for flowers, there are still plenty throughout the summer.

Sage-leaved Rock-rose

Pink Rock-rose

Azure Stonecrop

Alder

Viola

Broom

One of the incredible wind-battered trees on Stage 6a

Route Descriptions

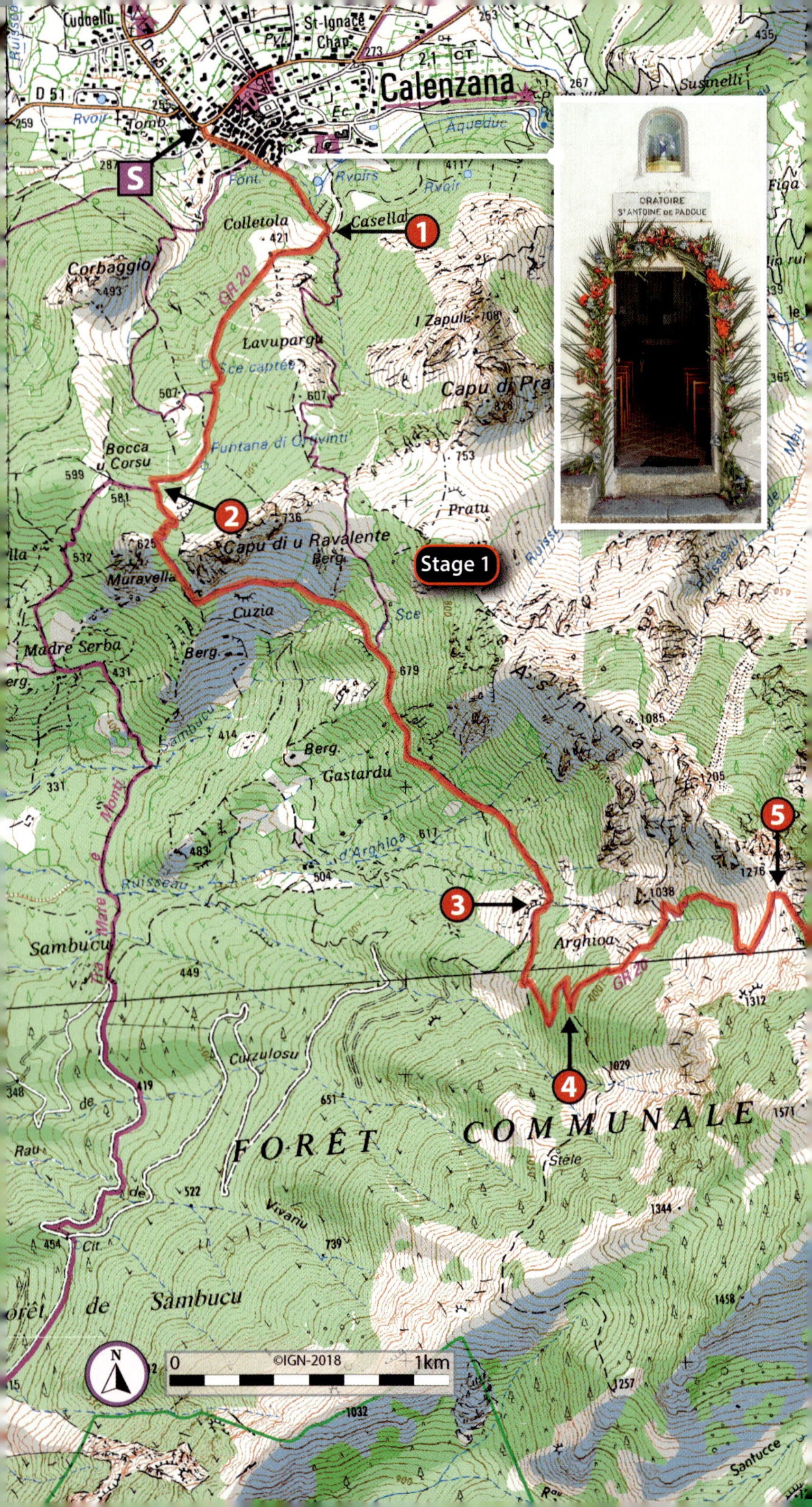

Calenzana
S
Stage 1
GR 20
Casella
Colletola
Corbaggio
Lavupargu
I Zapuli
Capu di Prat
Bocca u Corsu
Funtana di Cruvinti
Pratu
Capu di u Ravalente
Muravella
Cuzia
Madre Serba
Berg.
Gastardu
A S I N I N A
Arghioa
Sambucu
Curzulosu
FORÊT COMMUNALE
Stèle
Vivaru
Forêt de Sambucu
ORATOIRE ST ANTOINE DE PADOUE
©IGN-2018
0
1km
1
2
3
4
5

1
Capu di Ruia
Longa
Pardine
Acqua Freddula
Ruisseau
Frintogna
Erbajo
Tavulaghiu
Funtana di Mon
la Fratte
6
7
Ghiovu
Crête du Fucu
GR 20
Bocca di To
Refuge de l'Ortu di u Piobbu
Bonifatu Variant
liaison Bonifatu - GR 20
F
S
Stage 2

1

	N-S	S-N
Time	6:45	5:15
Distance (km)	11.9	11.9
Ascent (m)	1496	181
Descent (m)	181	1496
Max Alt (m)	1570	1570

The village of Calenzana

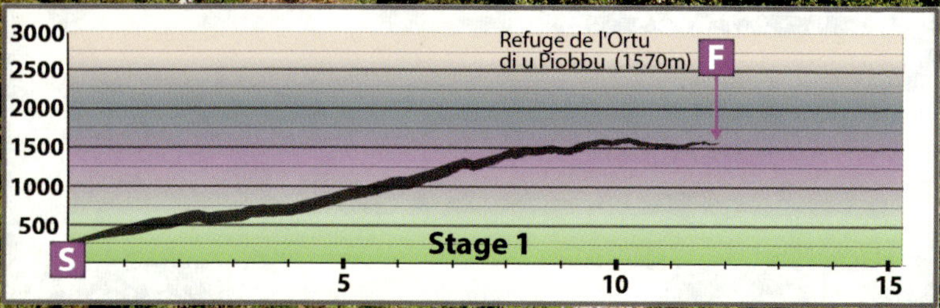

Calenzana to Refuge de l'Ortu di u Piobbu

1

Rising above the Corsican Maquis

For those walking N-S, this is a tough introduction to the GR20, involving a relentless ascent of almost 1500m. The scenery is lovely though, as you climb though the maquis out of Calenzana: one of the few times on the trek that you will experience this aromatic vegetation for which Corsica is renowned. As you get higher, the maquis fades away and you enter forest: unfortunately, forest fires have devastated parts of the hillsides in recent years. Eventually, the scenery at the pass known as Bocca u Saltu declares that you have arrived in the high mountains. You will not leave them until the end of the trek.

The climb is very long so it is wise to start early to avoid the hottest part of the day: if you reach Calenzana later in the day, then you may prefer to spend the night there and start the trek the following morning. Do not leave Calenzana without full water bottles.

At Waypoint No.6, you must scramble up a long section of rocks. This is a good initiation into the ways of the GR20: it is steep enough to test you but not as difficult as future challenges. Take your time as a fall could be serious. It is fair to say that if you cannot complete this section, the GR20 is no place for you. Do not worry if it takes you a long time: most people proceed faster over the tricky sections as they get further into the trek.

Refuge de l'Ortu di u Piobbu burnt down in 2019 and has not yet been replaced. The campsite, toilet blocks and kitchen remain operational. It is a busy place and those arriving later may find it difficult to secure a comfortable pitch.

Water: source in Calenzana near Oratoire St Antoine de Padoue; Funtana di Ortivinti (this is sometimes dry); source just after Refuge de l'Ortu di u Piobbu

Supplies/Meals: Calenzana, Refuge de l'Ortu di u Piobbu

Accommodation: Calenzana, Refuge de l'Ortu di u Piobbu

N-S

S **See Map 1**. From the Spar supermarket at the bottom of the village, walk up the main street. To start the GR20, TR just after the Bar/Pizzeria GR20 ('GR20'): alternatively, TL to head into the centre of the village. Shortly after turning right, bear left and climb through narrow streets (no waymarks). On the right, immediately before **Oratoire St Antoine**, there is a water source. Pass to the right of the chapel and keep SH, climbing on a path ('GR20').

1 0:20: TR at a junction. 20min later, keep SH at a junction. A few minutes later, pass a water source on the left: **Funtana di Ortivinti**.

2 1:00: TL at a junction ('GR20'): the path on the right is the Mare e Monti, another long-distance route. 10min later, cross a small col, **Bocca di u Ravalente (625m)**. Then start to descend: the views are magnificent. Soon the path climbs again.

3 1:40: Keep SH at a junction. Just afterwards, TL at a fork, taking a narrow path.

4 2:40: When the path bends right at some rocks, TL onto another path (waymark): easy to miss. After 10min, the gradient increases with some rocks to scramble over. After a while, the path splinters: keep following waymarks. Many of the trees have been destroyed by fire.

5 3:40: Reach the flat, grassy saddle at **Bocca u Saltu (1250m)**: TR (SE), descending over rocks. Soon, start to climb steeply again.

6 4:00: Scramble up a long section of steep rocks, following waymarks: watch your footing and stow your poles, leaving your hands free. Afterwards, descend for a few minutes and then start to climb again.

7 5:15: TL at a little grassy plateau and continue climbing on a clear path. After the climb, there is a straightforward descent. Soon the refuge can be seen on a rocky spur to the S. An undulating route now contours around the hillside.

F 6:45: After descending steeply over a few sections of rocks, climb briefly to arrive at **Refuge de l'Ortu di u Piobbu (1570m)**.

The beautiful scenery on the climb

S-N

F **See Map 1**. From Refuge de l'Ortu di u Piobbu, head NE and descend briefly. Then climb steeply over a few sections of rocks. The undulating route now contours around the hillside.

7 1:15: Descend to a little grassy plateau: TR and continue downhill. After climbing for a few minutes, scramble down a long section of rocks: watch your footing and stow your poles.

6 2:20: When you reach the end of the section of scrambling, continue descending. Then climb over rocks.

5 2:40: TL at the flat, grassy saddle at **Bocca u Saltu (1250m)**. When the path splinters, keep following waymarks. Soon, the gradient steepens with some rocks to scramble down.

4 3:10: When you arrive at another path, TR and descend on it.

3 3:45: Keep SH at two junctions. Continue descending for a while. Then climb to a small col, **Bocca di u Ravalente (625m)**: the views are magnificent. Cross the col and start to descend.

2 4:25: Keep SH at a junction, still descending. Shortly after passing a water source on the right (**Funtana di Ortivinti**), keep SH at a junction.

1 5:05: TL at a junction and descend on a path.

S 5:15: Arrive at a chapel (**Oratoire St Antoine**) at the entrance to **Calenzana**: to head to the supermarket, keep SH and descend through the narrow streets (no waymarks). After a few minutes, bear right. Shortly afterwards, TL at the Bar/Pizzeria GR20 and descend on a road: the Spar Supermarket is on the right. Alternatively, TR at Oratoire St Antoine to head into the centre of **Calenzana (273m)**.

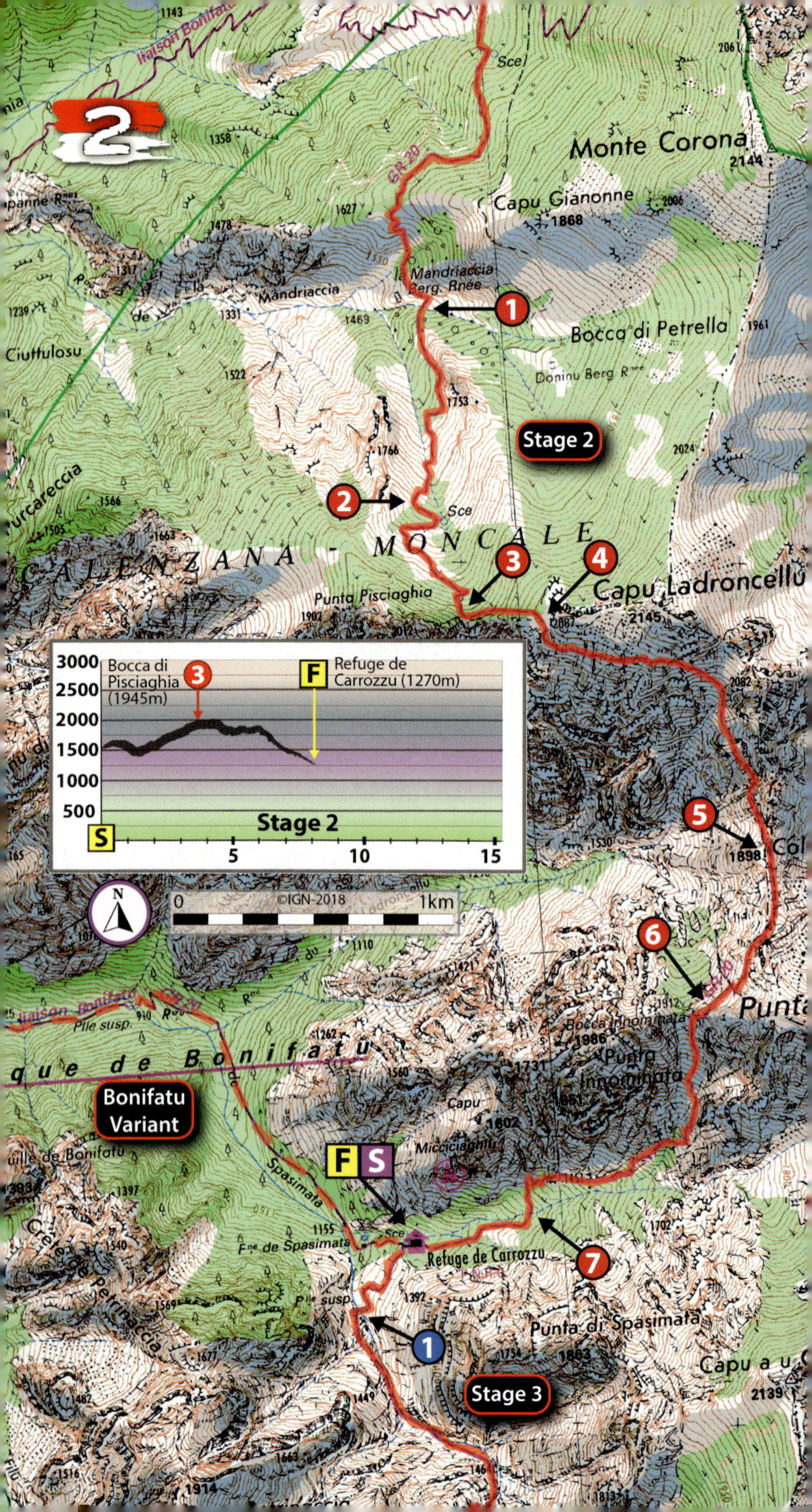

2
Monte Corona
Capu Gianonne
Mandriaccia
Bocca di Petrella
Ciuttulosu
Stage 2
CALENZANA - MONCALE
Punta Pisciaghia
Capu Ladroncellu
3000
2500
2000
1500
1000
500
Bocca di Pisciaghia (1945m)
Refuge de Carrozzu (1270m)
Stage 2
S
F
5
10
15
©IGN-2018
0
1km
Bonifatu Variant
Bocca Innominata
Punta Innominata
Capu Micciaghjolu
Refuge de Carrozzu
Spasimata
Punta di Spasimata
Stage 3

Refuge de l'Ortu di u Piobbu to Refuge de Carrozzu

2

The landscape softens after Col d'Avartoli

This magnificent stage is one of the highlights of the GR20. You will enter wild and remote terrain from which you will not emerge for many days. However, the terrain is significantly more difficult than that on Stage 1: the long, steep, challenging climb over boulders to Bocca di Pisciaghia is a shock to the system. Afterwards, there is an exquisite traverse on a balcony above the Cirque de Bonifatu: there are peaks everywhere you look and early season trekkers may be lucky enough to see them with a frosting of snow.

After a first descent, the route undulates as you scramble up and down rocks. The second descent is a long knee-jerker and you will arrive tired at the refuge. The camping area is small and rocky: the early bird may secure a pitch with shade amongst the trees.

The stage involves much scrambling over large rocks and boulders. It is difficult and you will move more slowly than you expect: exhausting stuff so early in the trek. Even the relatively 'level' sections are tough, with the route undulating relentlessly. The good news is that if you can finish this section, then you should be capable of completing the other sections of the GR20.

This stage enters exposed, high altitude terrain and should be avoided in bad weather or low visibility. In such conditions, you could use the Bonifatu Variant (see information box) which is lower and easier.

Water: source just after Refuge de l'Ortu di u Piobbu; stream at Waypoint No.1 (may be dry); source at Leccia Rossa (shortly before Waypoint No.3); Refuge de Carrozzu

Supplies/Meals: Refuge de Carrozzu; Bonifatu (off-route)

Accommodation: Refuge de Carrozzu; Bonifatu (off-route)

The view from Bocca di Pisciaghia

	N-S	S-N
Time	6:45	6:45
Distance (km)	8.2	8.2
Ascent (m)	770	1070
Descent (m)	1070	770
Max Alt (m)	2020	2020

N-S

S **See Map 1**. Head S on a path. Shortly afterwards, pass the refuge's water source. Just afterwards, the path climbs amongst rocks: it is initially hard to follow (cairns but no waymarks). Soon there are some faint waymarks. Keep SH, ignoring a faint path on the left, and descend gently among trees: the path is now clearer. 5min later, climb briefly. After a clearing with magnificent views, descend more steeply.

1 0:40: **See Map 2**. A few minutes later, cross a stream. Just afterwards, climb steeply: scramble across sections of boulders. Notice the pink granite rocks. After a level section, the climbing continues, with some scrambling over rocks. It gets steeper as you get higher.

2 1:40: After a tough climb, descend across rocks briefly. Then the route undulates for a few minutes and starts to climb steeply again, still over rocks: the waymarks are faint.

3 2:30: Arrive at **Bocca di Pisciaghia (1945m)**: TL and scramble up a ridge.

4 2:55: The path passes to the right of the ridge. Shortly afterwards, reach a spectacular col. Descend briefly and then traverse upwards along the hillside. Soon, start to descend steeply into the valley below. Afterwards, the stage is relentless, constantly dipping and rising so you are unable to get into any kind of rhythm. Climb steeply through a cleft in some rocks. A few minutes later, descend steeply again. Soon there is some tricky downward scrambling.

5 4:40: Climb again and reach **Col d'Avartoli (1898m)**: the terrain across the col is greener. TR and continue on a path. Shortly afterwards, TL at a faint junction and contour along the left of the ridge: do not bear right, descending through a gap in the rocks. 5min later, pass through another gap in the rocks and descend to the right of the ridge. Soon, climb yet again: there are few waymarks in this section.

6 5:10: Descend steeply. 10min later, arrive at **Bocca Innominata (1860m)**. Keep descending, following waymarks. The first part of the descent is rocky and unstable. After a while, follow waymarks down over rocks: the route is hard to follow.

7 6:30: Cross a small ravine on boulders and pick up a path on the other side (no waymarks).

F 6:45: Arrive at **Refuge de Carrozzu (1270m)**.

S-N

F **See Map 2**. Head E from Refuge de Carrozzu on a path.

7 0:15: Cross a small ravine on boulders and pick up a path on the other side (no waymarks). Follow waymarks up over rocks: the route is hard to follow. The last part of the climb is rocky and unstable.

6 2:30: Arrive at **Bocca Innominata (1860m)**: keep climbing steeply. Soon descend: there are few waymarks in this section. Climb again and pass through a gap in the rocks: now contour along the right of the ridge.

5 3:00: Bear left to cross **Col d'Avartoli (1898m)** and descend: the terrain across the col is much more barren. Afterwards, the stage is relentless, constantly dipping and rising so you are unable to get into any kind of rhythm. Soon there is some tricky upwards scrambling: climb steeply to a cleft in some rocks. Then descend on the other side of it. After a while, climb steeply out of the valley. Then traverse downwards across the hillside.

4 4:40: Climb briefly and reach a spectacular col. Shortly afterwards, the path bends left and you scramble down the spine of the ridge.

3 4:55: Arrive at **Bocca di Pisciaghia (1945m)**: TR and descend steeply over rocks (faint waymarks). Then the route undulates for a few minutes.

2 5:20: Climb across rocks briefly and then scramble steeply downwards. After a level section, the descent continues, scrambling over rocks.

1 6:05: Cross a stream. Climb steeply and then pass through a clearing with magnificent views. **See Map 1**. Afterwards, descend briefly. Soon the path is clearer as you climb gently among trees. After a while, ignore a faint path on the right. The waymarks are faint in this section. Eventually, descend among rocks: the route is hard to follow (cairns but no waymarks). Pass a water source on the right: fill up now as there is no source at the refuge itself.

S 6:45: Head N and soon arrive at **Refuge de l'Ortu di u Piobbu (1570m)**.

A trekker climbs away from Bocca di Pisciaghia

Bonifatu Variant

See Map 1. From Refuge de l'Ortu di u Piobbu, descend W on a path (yellow waymarks). Eventually, the path meets a track which you follow downwards.

2:40: Arrive at a river (620m): ford it using boulders. Take care if the water level is high. TL and climb on a path which follows the river SE. **See Map 2**. After a while, cross a bridge and continue uphill on the other side of the river.

4:45: Arrive at **Refuge de Carrozzu (1270m)**.

2

Stage 3
Old GR20:
Route Closed
F
S
1
2
3
4
5
Capu di a Marcia
Colonne di a Marcia
Bocca di Maghine
Lavu di a Muvrella
a Muvrella
Bocca di a Muvrella
Bocca di Stagnu
Plateau de Sta
Ancienne Station de Ski du Haut Asco
Refuge
GR20
Punta Stranciacone
Punta Missoghiu
Bocca Stranciacone
Capu di a Muvraghia
Boccala u Purtellu
Punta Rossa ou Pic Von Cube
Bocca Tumasginesca ou Col Perdu
Punta Minuta
Capu Rossu
Cirque de Trimbolacciu
l'Altare
Ghiarghia Minuta
Cascettoni ou Cirque de la Solitude
Petrinaccia

3
Monte Cintu
Micro centrale élect.
Berg. R.ne de Finusellu
Prise d'eau
Anc. stèle
Pont de Valentinu
FORÊT DE CAR
Manica
Piazzate
1973
Capu Borba
2305
Bocca Borba
2207
Tour Penchée
2116
Stage 4
Torre Manica
Punta Sellola
2592
Capu Ciuntrone
2656
Lac d'Argentu
MONTE CINTO
2706
Pnte des Éboulis
2607
Larghia
2380
Lac du Cinto
Petra Fisculi
©IGN-2018
0
1km
N
2
3
4
5

3

	N-S	S-N
Time	5:45	5:15
Distance (km)	6.1	6.1
Ascent (m)	819	667
Descent (m)	667	819
Max Alt (m)	1974	1974

Crossing between the two boccas: Monte Cinto can be seen in the background

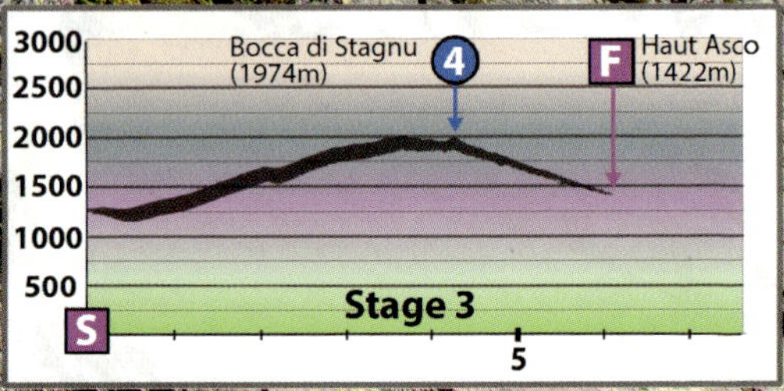

Refuge de Carrozzu to Haut Asco

3

The steep, rocky climb

Another spectacular but challenging stage. It starts with a long, steep climb to Bocca di a Muvrella where the views to the S are exquisite. A stunning traverse follows to the second high pass of the day, Bocca di Stagnu: you can see Monte Cinto, Corsica's highest mountain. Finally, there is a brutally steep descent to the little ski-station at Haut Asco (a.k.a. Asco Stagnu).

Take great care throughout this stage. The first section of the climb crosses exposed slabs which are slippery after rain: there are some fixed cables to assist. After Lac de la Muvrella, the final section of the climb is steep and rocky. On the traverse between the two boccas, there are some steep, exposed sections and sometimes it is easy to lose the waymarks.

After Waypoint No.1, there is no drinking water so fill up before leaving Refuge de Carrozzu. The excellent restaurant at Haut Asco is popular with trekkers for dinner and breakfast: you do not need to be a guest and there is a lovely outdoor terrace.

Water: stream at Waypoint No.1; source beside Refuge Asco Stagnu

Supplies/Meals: Refuge Asco Stagnu; restaurant at Hotel le Chalet; snack bar

Accommodation: Refuge Asco Stagnu; Hotel le Chalet

Escape/Access: Bus Vallée d'Ascu GR 20 runs a bus service between Haut Asco, Ponte Leccia and Calasima (May to September; book in advance): +33 (0)6 26 65 38 00; corsica-giru@bbox.fr; Facebook @busascugr20. You can use this service to skip Stage 4: from Calasima, you can walk to Auberge u Vallone (Stage 5a). From Ponte Leccia, you can catch a train to Bastia or Ajaccio. Bus Vallée d'Ascu GR 20 can also take you to other places in Corsica (including airport and ports), if booked in advance.

N-S

S **See Map 2.** Head SW from the refuge. Shortly after a heli-pad, keep SH at a junction ('Asco').

1 0:15: Cross the suspension bridge over Ruisseau de Spasimata. Then start to climb steeply, scrambling over rocks: the route makes its way up the valley above the stream. Sometimes there are chains and cables to assist.

2 2:25: **See Map 3**. After a long climb, arrive on a little plateau: TR and follow waymarks upwards. Shortly afterwards, pass the pretty **Lac de la Muvrella** on the left: the water of the lake is not drinkable. Just afterwards, scramble down some rocks. Shortly afterwards, start climbing steeply over rocks.

3 3:25: Arrive at the wonderfully narrow **Bocca di a Muvrella (1960m)**: keep SH following waymarks. Descend and shortly, scramble down a very steep rock: take great care. Continue descending steeply, often over boulders. TL at a faint junction (easy to miss) and climb again.

4 4:00: Arrive at **Bocca di Stagnu (1974m)**: you can see Monte Cinto and the territory crossed on Stage 4. Cross the bocca and descend SE on a steep path: watch your footing on the rocks.

5 5:40: TL onto a track. A few metres later, TR at a sign for 'Refuge Asco Stagnu'.

F 5:45: Soon afterwards, arrive in **Haut Asco (1422m)**.

3

Approaching Bocca di Stagnu

S-N

F **See Map 3**. From Refuge Asco Stagnu, pick up a path climbing W through trees. Soon, TL on a track.

5 0:05: Shortly afterwards, TR and climb on a path through trees. After a while, the route becomes rocky and challenging with sections of scrambling.

4 2:30: Arrive at **Bocca di Stagnu (1974m)**: you can see Monte Cinto and the territory crossed on Stage 4. Cross the bocca and descend NW following waymarks. After a while, start to climb steeply, often over boulders. As you approach the next bocca, scramble up a very steep rock: take great care.

3 3:05: Arrive at the wonderfully narrow **Bocca di a Muvrella (1960m)**: descend S. The route is steep and there are large rocks to clamber down. After scrambling up some rocks, pass the pretty **Lac de la Muvrella** on the right: the water of the lake is not drinkable.

2 3:35: Soon afterwards, TL at a little plateau and descend. The going is tough and steep and there are sections of scrambling: sometimes there are chains and cables to assist. Eventually, the route makes its way down a valley above a stream.

1 4:55: **See Map 2**. Cross the suspension bridge over Ruisseau de Spasimata. Afterwards, climb on a path. Keep SH at a junction. Shortly afterwards, pass a heli-pad.

S 5:15: Just afterwards, arrive at **Refuge de Carrozzu (1270m)**.

4
Old GR20: Route Closed
Stage 4
Stage 5a
Stage 5b
Albertacce Escape
F S
1
2
6
0
1km
©IGN 2018
Punta Rossa ou Pic Von Cube
Bocca Tumasginesca ou Col Perdu
Cirque
e Cascetto ou Cirque de la Solitude
l'Altare
Bocca Minuta
GR 20
Refuge Tighiettu
Capu Tighiettu
Serra di Mori
Ravin du Tramgacone
Pippaghiu
Berg. de Ballone
Breche d'Astratella
Capu Ucellu
Astratella
Serra Pianella
Orba
Ravin
la Grotte des Anges
Berg. de Prugnoli
Foggiale
Licciola
Bocca Rossa
Capu

Haut Asco to Refuge Tighiettu

4

Descending the Monte Cinto summit ridge

This is probably the 'Queen Stage' of the entire GR20 as it takes you almost to the summit of Monte Cinto (2706m), the highest mountain in Corsica. A long, tough climb brings you onto the ridge just below the summit: from there, it is only a short climb (off-route) to the top and most trekkers take the opportunity to stand on the roof of Corsica. Afterwards, descend SW along the spectacular summit ridge: the views are epic. After crossing another bocca, the descent to the refuge is a long, rocky 'knee-jerker'. From start to finish, the scenery is sublime so pray for a clear day.

This route is challenging and often exposed. On the climb, there are long sections of scrambling: often there are fixed cables to assist. On the final approach to the summit ridge, you must climb a steep and unstable slope: leave a large gap between yourself and those above you to avoid injury from rockfalls. This stage is unsuitable for those who have a fear of heights. As this is an exposed high altitude route, you should avoid it in bad weather or low visibility. Snow often lies on sections of this route well into June: in such conditions, crampons and an ice-axe may be advisable.

This stage is a relatively new addition to the GR20. The route was changed after bad weather and landslides in 2016 tragically killed seven walkers on the legendary old route through the Cirque de la Solitude. Many maps still show this old route but waymarks have been removed and you should not, under any circumstances, attempt it. In any case, many feel that the new route is more scenic.

Water: Ruisseau du Tighiettu and Ruisseau de Stranciacone on the climb; Ruisseau de Crucetta on the descent; Refuge Tighiettu

Supplies/Meals: Refuge Tighiettu

Accommodation: Refuge Tighiettu

The view on the descent towards Refuge Tighiettu

	N-S	S-N
Time	7:45	7:15
Distance (km)	9.4	9.4
Ascent (m)	1265	1004
Descent (m)	1004	1265
Max Alt (m)	2607	2607

N-S

S **See Map 3**. From the front of the hotel, head SE across a parking area. Pick up a signed path heading through forest: there are tantalising views of the high peaks between the trees. 15min later, cross a stream on rocks.

1 0:40: Cross a footbridge over a torrent. Just afterwards, start to scramble upwards: this section is very tough and often there are cables/chains to assist. Eventually, the scrambling gives way to a relentless slog up a steep shale slope.

2 2:30: Arrive at a magnificent plateau with amazing views back down the valley. Continue SH, following waymarks and cairns, across a section of rocks. Soon the shale continues.

3 3:15: Pass a superb viewpoint above **Lac d'Argentu**. 5min later, descend briefly to a saddle: often snow lies here late into the season. Then climb again on a clear path. Soon, bear left and scramble upwards.

4 4:30: Arrive at **Pointe des Éboulis (2607m)**. To climb Monte Cinto, see the information box. To continue on the GR20, cross the ridge and then descend SW on a path which soon runs down the crest of it. The shale terrain is unstable so watch your footing. The shimmering Lac du Cinto sits below to the S.

5 5:10: Traverse a rocky slope: there is no path. 10min later, scramble briefly up some rocks and arrive at **Bocca Crucetta (2456m)**: cross over and descend W on a steep shale path.

6 6:00: **See Map 4**. The path gets steeper and soon you descend over rocks: scrambling is required. 1hr later, cross a little stream (which may be dry). Shortly afterwards, pass a pretty waterfall on the left with a rock-pool.

F 7:45: Arrive at **Refuge Tighiettu (1683m)**. The setting of the refuge is lovely, giving wonderful views down the valley.

4

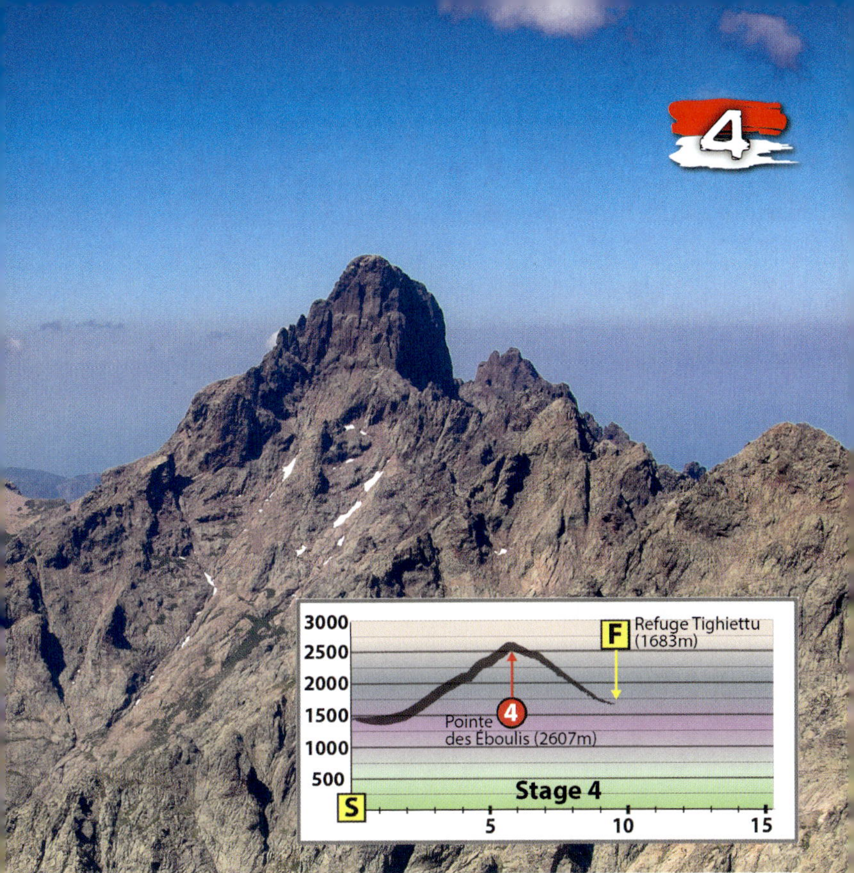

S-N

F **See Map 4**. From Refuge Tighiettu, head E on a path. Shortly afterwards, TL at a junction. Pass a pretty waterfall on the left with a lovely rock-pool. Shortly afterwards, cross a little stream (which may be dry). Soon the route becomes more difficult: as you climb over rocks, some scrambling is required.

5 3:00: **See Map 3**. Cross **Bocca Crucetta (2456m)**. Just afterwards, scramble down some rocks. Then traverse a rocky slope: there is no path. The shimmering Lac du Cinto sits below to the S. Soon climb NE on a path which runs up the crest of a ridge: the shale terrain is unstable so watch your footing.

4 3:50: Arrive at **Pointe des Éboulis (2607m)**. To climb Monte Cinto, see the information box. To continue on the GR20, cross the ridge and descend N. Soon scramble steeply downwards: take great care.

3 4:45: Pass a superb viewpoint above **Lac d'Argentu**: often snow lies here late into the season. Continue descending over shale slopes, following waymarks and cairns.

2 5:15: Arrive at a magnificent plateau with amazing views down the valley. Follow waymarks NW and continue descending. Soon descend a steep shale slope: watch your footing. Afterwards, enter the first of a long series of downwards scrambles: this section is very tough and often there are cables/chains to assist.

1 6:45: Cross a footbridge over a torrent. 15-20min later, cross a stream on rocks.

S 7:15: Arrive in **Haut Asco (1422m)**.

4

S-N walkers climbing towards Pointe des Éboulis

Ascent of Monte Cinto

1.5hr return trip from Pointe des Éboulis

At Waypoint No.4, head E and follow a waymarked path up the ridge. Soon, bear right and descend along the S side of the ridge. Then climb to a smaller summit (2651m). Afterwards, TR and descend across boulders. After a while, TL and scramble steeply up rocks. Finally, after an easier climb up the ridge, arrive on the summit of Monte Cinto (2706m). Afterwards, retrace your steps to Pointe des Éboulis.

Refuge Tighiettu to Auberge u Vallone

5a

A short walk alongside a beautiful stream with lovely waterfalls and rock-pools. Many take it slowly and cool down in the refreshing water. The views to the S are fabulous.

Auberge u Vallone is privately owned and well run so it is a popular stopping point. The plates of cheese and cold meats served at lunchtime are very tasty. The beer is also cold! Try to snag one of the magnificent camping pitches close to the stream (E of the auberge) where there are some more lovely rock-pools. The path is rocky but well-defined. Navigation is straightforward.

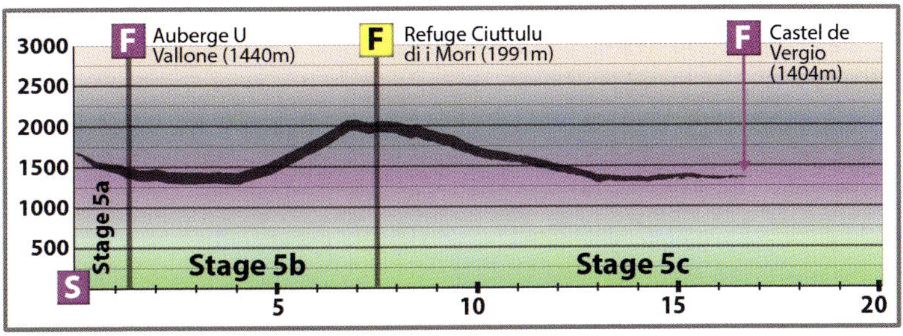

Water: the path follows a stream all the way but it may be dry later in the season; source at Auberge u Vallone (beside the shower block)

Supplies/Meals: Auberge u Vallone

Accommodation: Auberge u Vallone

Escape/Access: a path leads to Calasima (2.5hr; 7km) and Albertacce (3.75hr; 12km): see 'Albertacce Escape' below. From Calasima, Bus Vallée d'Ascu GR 20 runs a bus service to Ponte Leccia (May to October; book in advance): +33 (0)6 26 65 38 00; corsica-giru@bbox.fr; Facebook @busascugr20. From Ponte Leccia, you can catch a train to Bastia or Ajaccio. For S-N walkers wishing to avoid Stage 4, Bus Vallée d'Ascu GR 20 also travels to Haut Asco. From Albertacce, Autocars Cortenais runs a bus to Corte or Col de Verde: mid-may to mid-October; +33 (0)6 20 17 17 55; autocars.corte@wanadoo.fr

5a

	N-S	S-N
Time	0:30	0:45
Distance (km)	1.3	1.3
Ascent (m)	0	243
Descent (m)	243	0
Max Alt (m)	1683	1683

N-S

S **See Map 4**. From Refuge Tighiettu, head SE down the hillside towards the toilet: shortly after it, pick up a faint path on the left. Soon afterwards, TR onto the waymarked GR20. Alternatively, from the refuge, you can head back along the path of Stage 4 until you come to a junction: TR

1 0:10: Cross a stream beside a waterfall and pretty rock-pool. 15min later, ford the stream again.

F 0:35 Arrive at **Auberge u Vallone (1440m)**.

S-N

S **See Map 4**. From Auberge u Vallone, head N on a path. 15min later, ford the stream.

1 0:35: Cross the stream beside a waterfall and pretty rock-pool.

F 0:45: Arrive at **Refuge Tighiettu (1683m)**. The setting of the refuge is lovely, giving wonderful views down the valley.

Albertacce Escape

Head SE from Auberge u Vallone on a path (yellow waymarks) which soon fords the stream. Afterwards, head S on a rocky track used by vehicles serving the auberge. After a water tank, TR onto a path (yellow waymarks). When the path meets a track, keep on the path. When you meet the track a second time, head downhill on it. When it becomes a tarmac road, follow it all the way to Calasima (1095m) which is supposedly the highest village in Corsica. For Albertacce (860m), where there are some cafés and a gîte, keep following the road.

One of the rock-pools near Auberge u Vallone

Capu Tafunatu
5b
F S
Refuge Ciuttulu di i Mori
P.N.R.C.
Bocca di Foggiale
1962
Stage 5b
GR 20
Punta di Tula
Funtana di Monti Nielli
Berg. de Tula Rnes
Bafanina
GR 20
Ghiarghie
Stage 5c
Raviñ de
1656
1601
FORÊ
Golo
Capu a e Piane
Berg. de Pratelle
Bocca di Guagnarola
DE VALDU NIELLU
Capu di a Merla
1796
Casc.
Mare
Berg. de Radule
GR 20
Pnte de Cricche
2057
Zone Protegee
le Fer à Cheval
Calamalzi
Col de Vergio
©IGN-2018
0
1km
1
2
3

Auberge u Vallone to Refuge Ciuttulu di i Mori

5b

Refuge Ciuttulu di i Mori has a fabulous location below Paglia Orba

Although this is an easier walk than previous stages, the scenery is still wonderful. After leaving the auberge, the short, easy descent through forest is a delight in the cool of the morning: the slopes are coated with bright yellow broom flowers in early summer. A climb to Bocca di Foggiale follows: the path becomes increasingly rocky as you gain height. Continue climbing after the bocca and contour around the slopes on a magnificent balcony to Refuge Ciuttulu di i Mori which has one of the finest locations on the GR20: there are grassy tent pitches.

Although this stage is not as difficult as some, there are still steep, rocky sections on the climb: you will need to scramble in places and follow waymarks carefully. The sun hits the slopes of the climb early in the day, and there is no shade, so it is wise to start early.

If you have energy to spare (and a head for heights), you could climb to the summit of Paglia Orba (2525m), just NE of Refuge Ciuttulu di i Mori. The route climbs to Col des Maures and then heads NE up the ridge to the summit: take care as there is some very difficult scrambling on the ridge.

Water: stream at Waypoint No.1; source at Refuge Ciuttulu di i Mori

Supplies/Meals: Refuge Ciuttulu di i Mori

Accommodation: Refuge Ciuttulu di i Mori

	N-S	S-N
Time	3:30	3:00
Distance (km)	6.2	6.2
Ascent (m)	716	165
Descent (m)	165	716
Max Alt (m)	2041	2041

S-N trekkers descending to Bocca di Foggiale

5b

N-S

S **See Map 4**. Find the GR20 path just to the W of the auberge: head S down the valley. The clear path descends at first and then undulates gently.

1 0:35: Ford a stream on boulders.

2 1:00: Start climbing. **See Map 5b.** After 40min, scramble up sections of rocks.

3 2:50: TR at **Bocca di Foggiale (1962m)** and continue climbing: here the terrain changes from rock and trees to grass and low shrubs. 20min later, the refuge comes into view.

F 3:30: Arrive at **Refuge Ciuttulu di i Mori (1991m)**.

S-N

F **See Map 5b.** From Refuge Ciuttulu di i Mori, head E past the camp-ground on a path which soon climbs. After a while, start to descend.

3 0:40: TL at **Bocca di Foggiale (1962m)** and continue descending: here the terrain changes from grass and low shrubs to rock and trees.

2 1:55: **See Map 4**. Eventually, the path levels and undulates through the forest.

1 2:25: Ford a stream on boulders. Soon afterwards, start to climb.

S 3:00: Arrive at **Auberge u Vallone (1440m)**.

5c

	N-S	S-N
Time	3:30	4:15
Distance (km)	9.1	9.1
Ascent (m)	125	712
Descent (m)	712	125
Max Alt (m)	1991	1991

One of the magnificent rock-pools along the River Golo

Refuge Ciuttulu di i Mori to Castel de Vergio

5c

Col des Maures and Paglia Orba seen from Stage 5c

This stage is a delight. As the path is better than those on previous stages, you may find yourself relaxing a little, spending more time looking at the incredible scenery and less time looking at your feet. The views after leaving the refuge, as you contour around the slopes, are exquisite: you may spot the Mediterranean to the W.

Soon, however, you will descend into the Golo valley with its many rock-pools and waterfalls: many trekkers cool down in the pools and picnic nearby. Eventually, the path enters forest and starts to undulate. After the remote territory of the previous days, the services at the quiet Castel de Vergio are very welcome. It may be possible to rent a donkey to carry your pack on subsequent stages: La Promenane (+33 (0)6 15 29 45 64; www.randonnee-ane-corse.com).

Although the path is rocky, it is clear and well-defined. The stage is generally well marked but occasionally, the route is hard to follow in the forest.

Water: River Golo: livestock nearby so it is wise to treat the water; taps at Castel de Vergio

Supplies/Meals: snacks at Bergerie de Radule; restaurant at Hotel Castel de Vergio; shop at the campsite

Accommodation: camping may be possible at Bergerie de Radule; Hotel/Gîte/Camping at Castel de Vergio

Escape/Access: Autocars Cortenais runs a bus from Castel de Vergio to Albertacce and Corte: mid-May to mid-October; +33 (0)6 20 17 17 55; autocars.corte@wanadoo.fr.

Mediterranean views shortly after leaving the refuge

N-S

S **See Map 5b**. Take the path heading SW from the refuge which traverses beautifully across the slopes. After 20min, climb briefly to a large cairn where there are superb views of the Mediterranean. Then descend on a good path.

1 1:25: Pass a magnificent waterfall with a spectacular mountain backdrop. Shortly afterwards, keep SH at a junction. 15-20min later, cross a bridge over the river: Then, TR and descend alongside the river: the path is rocky and uneven.

2 2:00: TR and cross the river again on another bridge. Then keep following the path downstream. 10min later, climb briefly and pass through the buildings of **Bergerie de Radule**. Afterwards, descend again, contouring around the hillside.

3 2:45: Cross a boulder field, following cairns: there are few waymarks.

F 3:30: **See Map 6a**. TL and walk alongside a road for a few minutes to **Hotel Castel de Vergio (1404m)**. The campsite and grocery store are slightly further down the road.

5c

S-N

F **See Map 6a**. From the campsite at Castel de Vergio, walk W along the road. A few minutes after passing the hotel, TR on a path.

3 0:45: **See Map 5b**. Cross a boulder field, following cairns: there are few waymarks. Afterwards, the path undulates through the trees. After a while, climb briefly and pass through the buildings of **Bergerie de Radule**. Afterwards, descend briefly and then start the main climb of the stage.

2 1:30: Cross the river on a bridge. Then follow the path upstream: it is rocky and uneven. 20-30min later, cross another bridge over the river. 20min later, keep SH at a junction.

1 2:30: Shortly afterwards, pass a magnificent waterfall with a spectacular mountain backdrop. Afterwards, continue climbing on a good path. Eventually, reach a large cairn where there are superb views of the Mediterranean. Now the path contours beautifully around the slopes.

S 4:15: 20min after the cairn, arrive at **Refuge Ciuttulu di i Mori (1991m)**: there are lovely grassy tent pitches.

Stage 5c
F S
0 ©IGN-2018 1km
Castellu di Vergio
Capu di Vergio
Téleskis
Bocca â Manuella
Stage 6a
Pont du Renaghiu
Pont de Cuccagna
Caroline
FORÊT
Crête de Scupertu
Capu a Rughia
1
2
Bocca San Pedru
Sentier
Berg. de Custole
Terricci
3
4
Serra San
GR 20
Route to Cristinacce
de la Mente
Faeta
u Tritore
Berg. de Capelacce
Piazzilellu Berg.
Sce de Macciochi
Capu di Farinetu

6a
de Mezzanule
Frascaghiu
Scie de Serriera
VALDU
VALDU
Crête d'Orsu
Capu a u Tozzu
Bocca â Stazzona
Lac de Nino
Bocca â Reta
Ravin de Curia
Ravin de l'Inzecche
Cimatella
Bergeries de Vaccaghia (1621m)
F
F
Refuge de Manganu (1601m)
3000
2500
2000
1500
1000
500
S
Stage 6a
Stage 6b
5
10
15
20

The incredible viewpoint above Lac de Nino (after Waypoint No.5)

Castel de Vergio to Bergeries de Vaccaghia

6a

The stone oratory at Bocca San Pedru

This stage is completely different from the rest of the GR20, crossing a wonderland of green pastures around the famous Lac de Nino: it is a clear highlight of the trek. The first hour involves a shady traverse through aromatic pine forest: a relief on a hot Corsican day. Afterwards, climb to Bocca San Pedru and enjoy a sustained ridge walk with amazing views to the N. After a staggering viewpoint above Lac de Nino, walk along the grassy shores of the lake. Finally, pass through lovely pastures on the way to Bergeries de Vaccaghia.

The path along the ridge undulates and is tiring: sections of it are rocky and uneven. Also, after Bergerie des Inzecche, the route is sometimes difficult underfoot. Navigation is generally straightforward as the markings are good. However, watch out for the junction at Waypoint No.3 which is easy to miss. It is forbidden to camp at Lac de Nino and there is weed around the lake's fringes, making swimming difficult.

Water: after Waypoint No.5, there is normally water in the streams (there is livestock nearby so it is wise to filter/treat it before drinking); source off-route along the S side of Lac de Nino at a little shrine: do not drink from the lake itself; source at Bergeries de Vaccaghia.

Supplies/Meals: Bergerie des Inzecche; Bergeries de Vaccaghia

Accommodation: Bergeries de Vaccaghia

Escape/Access: the village of Cristinacce is a 3-4hr walk SW from Bocca San Pedru (Waypoint No.2). Also, from Bergeries de Vaccaghia, an alternative path (heading NE down the Tavignano valley) leads to Corte (21km; 7-8hr).

N-S

S **See Map 6a.** From the campsite at Castel de Vergio, TL down the road. Shortly, just after an information board, TR onto a path and descend through trees. Soon the path levels, leading you on a delightfully easy stroll through the forest: stroll is not a word often used to describe the GR20!

1 1:10: TR at a junction: the waymark here is slightly confusing. Now start climbing: the path is stony and uneven but not too steep.

2 1:35: TL at **Bocca San Pedru (1452m)** and continue climbing. There is a prominent stone oratory at the bocca. A few minutes later, pass some much-photographed trees which have been shaped by the prevailing winds.

3 2:25: Turn sharp right at a junction: easy to miss. 15min later, keep climbing past a little gap with magnificent views.

4 3:10: Cross another narrow gap to the S side of the ridge: descend briefly and then climb again. TR at a saddle and head briefly up the crest of the ridge. Soon the path passes along the right side of the ridge again, below the summit of Capu a u Tozzu.

5 3:40: Keep SH across **Bocca â Reta (1883m)** and enter magnificent pastures. 10-15min later, arrive at a viewpoint overlooking the stunning Lac de Nino: keep SH on the path, descending towards the lake. The path splinters frequently: follow the GR20 waymarks which lead you around the N side of **Lac de Nino (1743m).**

6 4:30: TL at a fork and head towards farm buildings. **See Map 6b**. 5min later, pass below **Bergerie des Inzecche (1761m)**: if you climb a few metres to the bergerie, you can buy cheese. Just afterwards, the path bends sharply right. 5min later, cross a stream. Afterwards, the route alternates between challenging rocky sections and lovely sandy paths.

7 5:15: Cross a stream.

F 5:45: Head around a corner to arrive at **Bergeries de Vaccaghia (1621m)**.

Stage 6a crosses many beautiful pastures

	N-S	S-N
Time	5:45	5:15
Distance (km)	15.3	15.3
Ascent (m)	566	349
Descent (m)	349	566
Max Alt (m)	1883	1883

S-N

F **See Map 6b**. From Bergeries de Vaccaghia, head N on a path.

7 0:30: Cross a stream. Afterwards, the route alternates between challenging rocky sections and lovely sandy paths. Eventually, cross another stream. 5min later, pass below **Bergerie des Inzecche (1761m)**: if you climb a few metres to the bergerie, you can buy cheese.

6 1:30: 5min later, keep SH at a junction. Soon, follow the GR20 waymarks around the N side of **Lac de Nino (1743m)**. After the lake, climb W: take care to follow waymarks as the path splinters frequently. After a superb viewpoint overlooking the lake, continue W on a path: cross magnificent pastures.

5 2:35: Keep SH across **Bocca â Reta (1883m)** and descend along the left side of the summit of Capu a u Tozzu. When you reach the crest of a ridge, head down it briefly. Soon TL at a saddle and descend. Then climb briefly and cross a narrow gap to the N side of the ridge. Continue descending.

3 3:25: TL at a junction and continue descending. After a while, pass some much-photographed trees which have been shaped by the prevailing winds.

2 3:50: A few minutes later, reach the prominent stone oratory at **Bocca San Pedru (1452m)**: TR and continue descending. The path is stony and uneven but not too steep.

1 4:05: TL at a junction. Now enjoy a delightfully easy stroll through the forest. After a while, climb to an information board: TL onto a road.

S 5:15: Shortly afterwards, arrive at the campsite and grocery store at **Castel de Vergio (1404m)**. The hotel is a little further along the road.

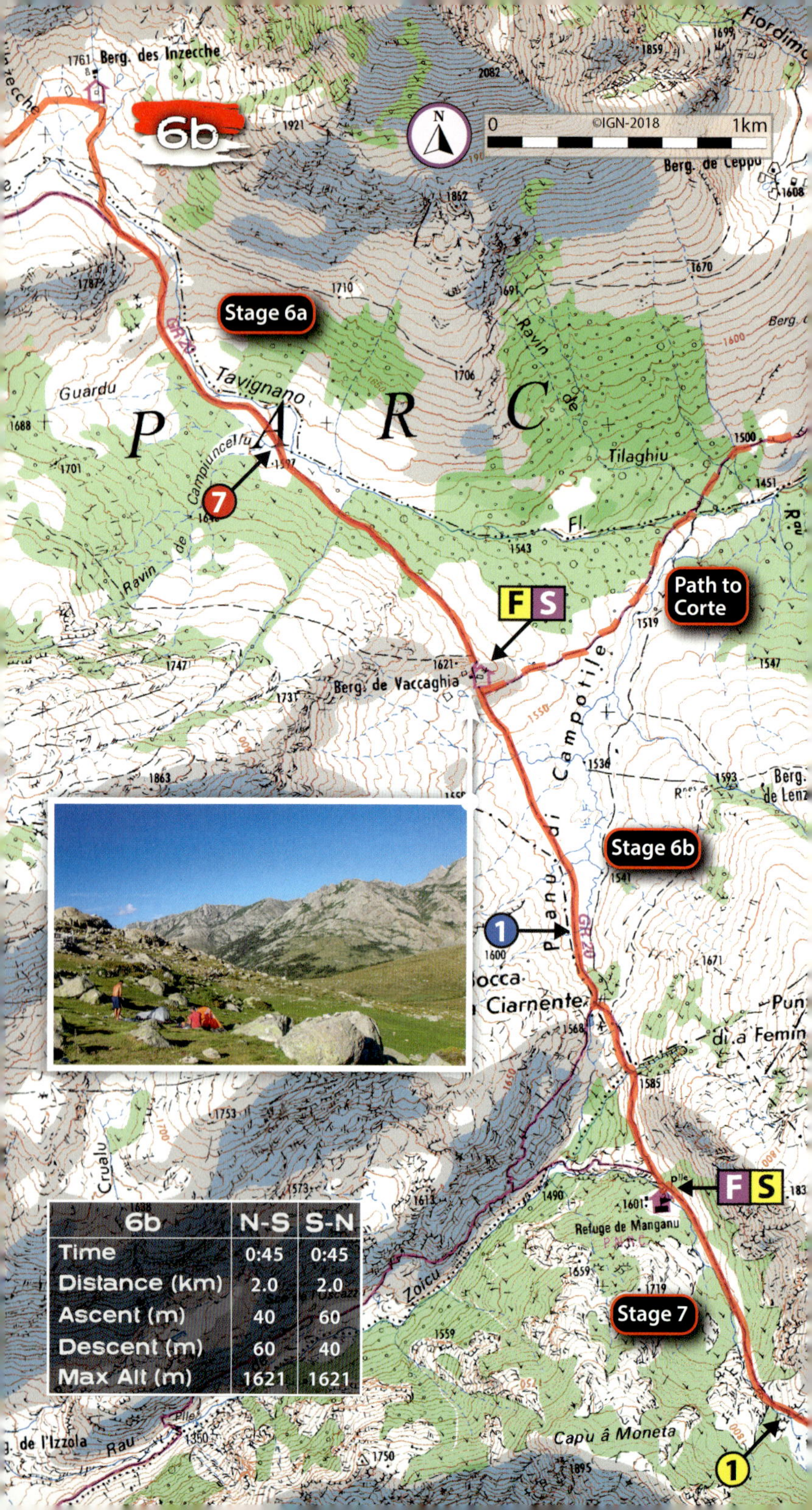

6b	N-S	S-N
Time	0:45	0:45
Distance (km)	2.0	2.0
Ascent (m)	40	60
Descent (m)	60	40
Max Alt (m)	1621	1621

Bergeries de Vaccaghia to Refuge de Manganu

6b

Refuge de Manganu

Refuge de Manganu (at one end of this stage) is clearly visible from Bergeries de Vaccaghia (at the other end): they are separated by a short walk across grassy pastures. Refuge de Manganu has a beautiful setting and there are some lovely grassy camping pitches. Terrain and navigation are straightforward.

N-S

S **See Map 6b**. From the dining area of the bergerie, follow a waymarked path SE and descend to the base of the valley.

1 0:15: Start to climb. A few minutes later, the path levels: keep SH at a junction.

F 0:45: Cross a bridge and arrive at **Refuge de Manganu (1601m)**.

S-N

F **See Map 6b**. From Refuge de Manganu, head back across the bridge. Immediately afterwards, TL on an undulating path. Soon descend towards the base of the valley.

1 0:25: Head N across the valley floor. Soon, start to climb.

S 0:45: Arrive at **Bergeries de Vaccaghia (1621m)**.

Water: streams along the route (livestock nearby so it is wise to filter/treat water before drinking); source at Refuge de Manganu

Supplies/Meals: Refuge de Manganu

Accommodation: Refuge de Manganu

Stage 7
CAPU A I SORBI
POINTE DES SEPT LACS
LAC DE CAPITELLO
CAPITELLO
Brèche de Goria
Brèche de Sorbo
Bocca alle Porte
PUNTA ALLE PORTE
Brèche de Capitello
CRÊTE DE RINELLA
Bocca a Soglia
LAC DE M
GR 20
©IGN-2018
0
1km
N
1
2
3
4
5
6
7
Costa di Catalina
Grotta a l'Orsa
Berg. Rnée
Querci
de Trayette
Bocca Forca

7
LAC DE SCAPUCCIOLI
LAVU BELLEBONE
Monte Pozzolo
LAC DE POZZOLO
Aiguille noire de Stozzo Vecchio
A MANICCIA
LAC DE RINOSO
Col de Rinoso
Bocca Muzzella
8
PUNTA MUZZELLA
Scafone
Misogi
Rasino
Laggiarello
Stazzanelli
Valle di Petra Piana
F
S
Chiosu
Refuge de Petra Piana
GR 20
Source Belle Cave
Bergeries de Gialgo
Stage 8
Bocca Manganello
1
2
Fnt de Stazzanelli
POINTE MURACE
l'Orso Franco
Stage v8
Bergeries de Bassitone
Tassiccione
Serra Bianca
Etang de Gialicatapiano
Giargione
PNTE DE PINZI CORBINI
Bocca a Meta
Largiola
Fontaine Largiola
Bergeries de Baccialojo
PNTE DE BACCIALOJO
SERRA DI TENDA
Teghie Nere
CRETE DE MURATA
Terriccione
Scopiccioli
C O R S E

7

Incredible scenes as you walk the ridge

Refuge de Manganu to Refuge de Petra Piana

7

Refuge de Petra Piana

This challenging stage has some of the most difficult terrain on the GR20. Fortunately, however, it also has some of the most beautiful scenery. There are exceptional views throughout but the two magnificent lakes, Lac de Capitello and Lac de Melo, steal the show. There are also a number of stunning high passes to cross and an incredible ridge walk (arguably the finest on the GR20). In good conditions, this is a day that you will never forget.

This stage is very rocky throughout and involves probably the hardest scrambling on the GR20. There are long, steep climbs with boulders and slabs to scramble over. Approaching Bocca alle Porte, you climb a steep and unstable slope: leave a large gap between yourself and any person above to avoid injury from rock-falls. Afterwards, you must descend some very exposed, vertical sections of rocks with cables to assist: a fall would have serious consequences. After another steep climb (with some scrambling), there is a knee-jerking descent to the refuge. This stage is best avoided if you have a fear of heights.

Navigation can be tricky. As this is an exposed high altitude route, you should avoid it in bad weather or low visibility. Snow often lies on parts of the route well into June: in such conditions, crampons and an ice-axe may be advisable.

If you have energy to spare (and a head for heights), you could climb to the summit of Monte Rotondo (2622m), the second highest mountain on Corsica. Starting at Refuge de Petra Piana, the route climbs rocky slopes to the N. There is some scrambling involved and navigation is not easy. The return trip takes 4-5hr.

Water: there is no water on the route so fill up before leaving Refuge de Manganu; source at Refuge de Petra Piana

Supplies/Meals: Refuge de Petra Piana

Accommodation: Refuge de Petra Piana

Escape/Access: Paths from Brèche de Capitello and Bocca a Soglia lead N to Bergerie de Grottelle (4km; 2hr). From there, Autocars Cortenais runs a bus to Corte in high season: +33 (0)6 20 17 17 55; autocars.corte@wanadoo.fr. You can buy local foods at Bergerie de Grottelle

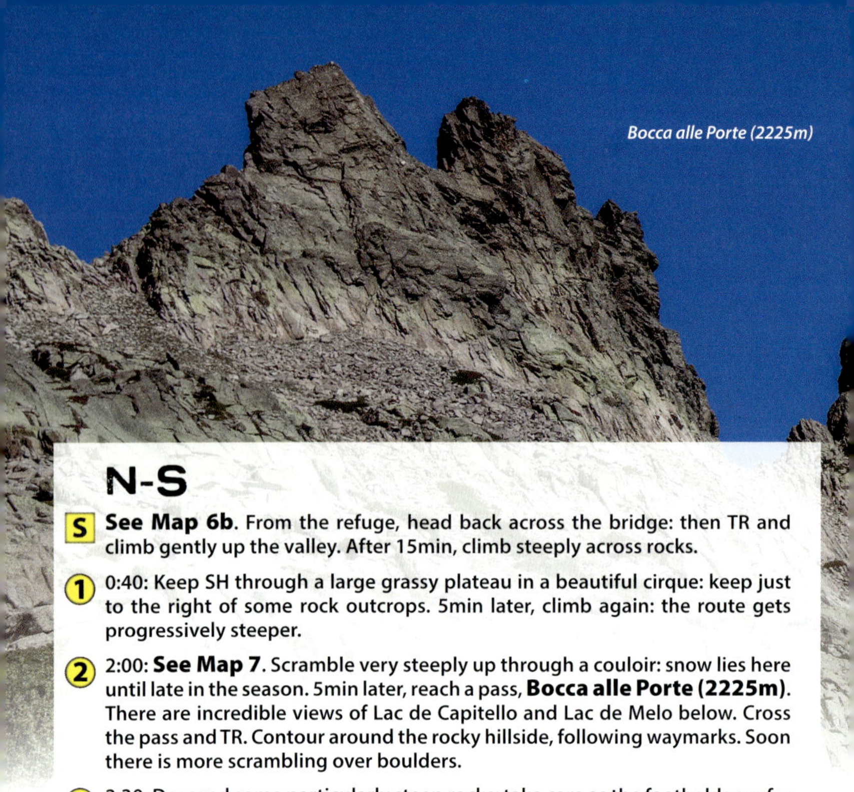

Bocca alle Porte (2225m)

N-S

S **See Map 6b**. From the refuge, head back across the bridge: then TR and climb gently up the valley. After 15min, climb steeply across rocks.

1 0:40: Keep SH through a large grassy plateau in a beautiful cirque: keep just to the right of some rock outcrops. 5min later, climb again: the route gets progressively steeper.

2 2:00: **See Map 7**. Scramble very steeply up through a couloir: snow lies here until late in the season. 5min later, reach a pass, **Bocca alle Porte (2225m)**. There are incredible views of Lac de Capitello and Lac de Melo below. Cross the pass and TR. Contour around the rocky hillside, following waymarks. Soon there is more scrambling over boulders.

3 2:30: Descend some particularly steep rocks: take care as the footholds are far apart. At times the waymarks are sporadic so watch out for cairns. 5-10min later, there are more fabulous views of Lac de Capitello. Shortly afterwards, descend a long vertical section of rocks which is protected by chains: a fall here would be very serious. Just afterwards, scramble steeply upwards.

4 2:55: Arrive at **Brèche de Capitello**, a little ledge where there is a junction. Ignore the path descending to the left which is the escape route to Bergerie de Grottelle (see above). Rather, keep SH along the right side of the ridge. Just afterwards, there is some more scrambling, followed by a short, steep descent. The following section of scrambling is very hard: take your time and wait for others to finish before commencing each part.

5 3:30: Arrive on the crest of the ridge: there are sublime views on both sides. Soon, TL at a junction beside some black rocks and continue along the ridge.

6 4:00: Towards the end of the ridge, the path bears left. Shortly afterwards, TR at **Bocca e Soglia (2052m)**: the path to the left is the second escape route to Bergerie de Grottelle (see above). Keep following waymarks, ignoring offshoots. The path works its way upwards, undulating relentlessly. Soon, cross long sections of boulders: follow waymarks carefully.

7 4:40: TR steeply up the hillside: easy to miss. 15min later, after a tough climb, keep SH over **Col de Rinoso (2150m)** and across a rocky plateau (cairns). Snow lies here late into the season. Soon afterwards, another lake, Lac de Rinoso, reveals itself below on the left. The waymarks here are quite far apart and are easy to lose.

8 5:40: Cross a plateau and keep SH, continuing to climb the rocky path. 5min later, cross **Bocca Muzzella (2206m)**: follow waymarks SE and descend across the rocky slopes. The final descent is very steep.

F 6:45: Arrive at **Refuge de Petra Piana (1842m)**. The views are spectacular but there is no shade.

	N-S	S-N
Time	6:45	6:15
Distance (km)	9.3	9.3
Ascent (m)	862	621
Descent (m)	621	862
Max Alt (m)	2225	2225

7

S-N

F **See Map 7**. From Refuge de Petra Piana, climb steeply NW.

8 1:30: A few minutes after crossing **Bocca Muzzella (2206m)**, follow waymarks through a plateau. Then continue descending: the waymarks are quite far apart and are easy to lose. Snow lies here late into the season. Soon, Lac de Rinoso, reveals itself below on the right. Cross another rocky plateau (cairns). Just afterwards, reach **Col de Rinoso (2150m)**: descend steeply.

7 2:10: TL and contour around the slopes on an undulating path. Soon, cross long sections of boulders: follow waymarks carefully. Afterwards, keep following waymarks, ignoring offshoots. TL at **Bocca e Soglia (2052m)**: the path to the right is an escape route to Bergerie de Grottelle (see above).

6 2:50: Shortly afterwards, the path bears right and heads along a ridge. There are sublime views on both sides. Bear right at a junction beside some black rocks and continue along the ridge.

5 3:20: The route leaves the crest of the ridge: the next section involves difficult scrambling so take your time and wait for others to finish each section before you commence. A short, steep climb is followed by some scrambling.

4 3:55: Arrive at **Brèche de Capitello**, a little ledge where there is a junction. Keep SH and ignore the path descending to the right which is another escape route to Bergerie de Grottelle (see above). Soon scramble downwards steeply. Just afterwards, climb a long vertical section of rocks which is protected by chains: a fall here would be very serious.

3 4:25: Soon climb some particularly steep rocks: take care as the footholds are far apart. At times, the waymarks are sporadic so watch out for cairns. Then there is more scrambling over boulders. Next contour around the rocky hillside, following waymarks.

2 5:00: TL to cross **Bocca alle Porte (2225m)**. Soon scramble very steeply down through a couloir: snow lies here until late in the season.

1 5:50: **See Map 6b**. Keep SH through a large grassy plateau in a beautiful cirque: towards the end of it, keep just to the left of some rock outcrops. Afterwards, descend steeply across rocks. After 10-15min, the gradient eases.

S 6:15: TL and cross a bridge to reach **Refuge de Manganu (1601m)**.

8	N-S	S-N
Time	4:45	5:30
Distance (km)	10.9	10.9
Ascent (m)	440	897
Descent (m)	897	440
Max Alt (m)	1842	1842

Refuge de Petra Piana to l'Onda

8

The route descends to the valley floor

It is fair to say that this is not the finest section of the GR20 but it is lovely all the same. A steep, scenic descent leads into beautiful forest which provides welcome relief from the Corsican heat. After a long walk beside Ruisseau de Manganello, take a break at Bergeries de Tolla. This is possibly the friendliest place on the entire trek: there is an excellent buvette which sells drinks and home-made bread, cheese and cold meats. They also have a cabin where you can stay and they may let you camp if you ask nicely.

After Bergeries de Tolla, continue descending alongside the stream: there are some beautiful rock-pools. After crossing a bridge, climb alongside another stream and more rock-pools: many trekkers cool down in them.

The campsite at l'Onda is one of the nicest on the GR20: there are plenty of grassy pitches. Hot meals and groceries are available at the bergerie next door. Refuge de l'Onda is a short climb above the bergerie: there are beds and a small kitchen but you will have to descend to the bergerie to buy a hot meal.

The first part of the descent is very steep and rocky. Otherwise, the terrain is straightforward. Navigation poses few difficulties. Take care if you are proposing to cool down in the rock-pools.

Many trekkers prefer to use the more difficult variant route (Stage v8) which is higher and more scenic.

Water: streams along the route; source in the camp-ground at l'Onda

Supplies/Meals: Bergeries de Tolla; l'Onda

Accommodation: small cabin at Bergeries de Tolla; Campsite and refuge at l'Onda

Escape/Access: a path from Waypoint No.4 leads to Tattone and Savaggio (see 'Tattone Escape' below). From both Savaggio and Tattone, there are trains to Ajaccio, Vizzavona or Bastia: request stops only so wave to the train driver. Savaggio has a campsite. Tattone has a campsite and gîte

N-S

S **See Map 7**. From the buildings of Refuge de Petra Piana, head SW through the campsite and pick up a waymarked path heading SW. A few minutes later, TL at a junction (easy to miss) and descend on a steep, rocky path: alternatively, keep SH for Stage v8. Follow waymarks when the path disappears.

1 0:35: Keep SH past an old building. Shortly afterwards, cross a stream. Afterwards, the path is clear but often rocky: it contours around the hillside, offering wonderful views of the valley. After a while, pass a beautiful waterfall.

2 1:25: Keep SH past a little cabin: the path continues to descend, gently now, through shady forest.

3 3:00: **See Map 8**. Arrive at **Bergeries de Tolla (1011m)**. From the bergerie, head downhill on the path.

4 3:10: After 10min, cross a bridge (Passerelle de Tolla) and climb on the other side. A few minutes later, TR, taking the higher of two tracks. 5-10min later, TR at a junction. The path follows the river for the time being and there are lots of rock-pools and waterfalls. The climb is gentle and shady. After a while, the path becomes rocky and the gradient increases. Soon, it becomes very faint: follow waymarks amongst the rocks and trees.

5 3:50: Ford a stream on rocks. Shortly afterwards, climb steeply.

F 4:45: Arrive at the camp-ground and bergerie at **l'Onda (1385m)**. Keep climbing for a few minutes to reach **Refuge de l'Onda (1431m)**.

Tattone Escape

7.6km; 3.25hr

Just after crossing Passerelle de Tolla (Waypoint No.4), descend E on a path (orange waymarks) beside Ruisseau de Manganello. Many walkers cool down in the rock-pools. After a while, the path becomes a track. At **Canaglia (720m)**, keep SH on a road: there is a restaurant in the hamlet. The road descends gently. Soon after crossing a stream, it climbs. About 1.5km later, TL on a track to head to Savaggio: when you reach the railway line, TR alongside it to go to the station and campsite/gîte. Alternatively, to head to Tattone, remain on the road: soon after crossing the railway tracks, TR on a track to find Tattone's station and campsite.

S-N

F **See Map 8**. From the camp-ground at l'Onda, descend N on a path.

5 0:40: Ford a stream on rocks. Afterwards, the route follows the river downstream and there are lots of rock-pools and waterfalls. The path is faint in places: follow waymarks amongst the rocks and trees.

4 1:10: TL at a junction. Shortly afterwards, cross a bridge (Passerelle de Tolla) and climb on the other side.

3 1:30: Pass **Bergeries de Tolla (1011m)**. Soon the path starts to climb again.

2 3:30: **See Map 7**. Keep SH past a little cabin: the path continues to climb. After a while, pass a beautiful waterfall.

1 4:30: Shortly after crossing a stream, keep SH past an old building. Follow waymarks when the steep, rocky path disappears.

S 5:30: TR at a junction. Shortly afterwards, arrive at **Refuge de Petra Piana (1842m)**. The views are spectacular but there is no shade.

8

Welcome shade in the forest

v8

Looking N along the ridge

Refuge de Petra Piana to l'Onda (Haute Route)

V8

The route follows the ridge-line at the top right of the picture

Scenically this official GR20 variant is superior to the main route (Stage 8). Instead of heading down into the valley, it leads you up along magnificent ridges with wide-ranging views. The disadvantage is that you won't get to resupply at Bergeries de Tolla or have the opportunity to cool down in the lovely rock-pools on Stage 8.

There is a small amount of scrambling but it is not as difficult as some other parts of the GR20. Otherwise, the terrain is straightforward. The route generally follows the ridge but S of Bocca a Meta, it can be hard to follow. As this is an exposed high altitude route, you should avoid it in bad weather or low visibility. In places, snow often remains well into June, sometimes making the route dangerous: in such conditions, crampons and an ice-axe may be advisable.

The campsite at l'Onda is one of the nicest on the GR20: there are plenty of grassy pitches. Hot meals and groceries are available at the bergerie next door. Refuge de l'Onda is above the bergerie: you will pass it on the way down to the camp-ground and bergerie. The refuge has beds and a small kitchen but you will have to descend to the bergerie to buy a hot meal.

If you wish to continue to Vizzavona without stopping at l'Onda, you could TR at Waypoint No.4 to pick up the Stage 9 path.

Water: none on the route so fill up before leaving Refuge de Petra Piana; source in the camp-ground at l'Onda

Supplies/Meals: Bergerie at l'Onda

Accommodation: Bergerie at l'Onda

GR20 trekkers climbing onto the ridge from Bocca Manganello

N-S

S **See Map 7**. From the buildings of Refuge de Petra Piana, head SW through the camping area and pick up a waymarked path heading SW. A few minutes later, keep SH at a junction (yellow waymarks): the path descending to the left is the main GR20 (Stage 8). Descend across a rocky slope. Then start to climb.

1 0:30: From **Bocca Manganello (1800m)**, head S up a ridge. Pass below the summit of **Pointe Murace (1921m)**. Then keep heading along the ridge.

2 1:30: Reach the summit of **Pointe de Pinzi Corbini (2021m)**. Then follow the rocky path S, down to **Bocca a Meta (1890m)**. Soon the route passes to the NE side of the ridge (yellow waymarks): there is some scrambling. The path drifts back to the right and climbs steeply to a gap: head up to the left. Afterwards, the path continues SE, often just off the crest of the ridge. The rocky path soon descends more steeply.

3 3:25: **See Map 8**. Arrive at **Bocca d'Oreccia (1427m)**: keep SH, climbing E up a spur. Once on the spur, TR and climb up its crest.

4 3:40: TL at a junction and descend. Soon arrive at **Refuge de l'Onda (1431m)**. Continue downhill to head to the camp-ground.

F 3:45: A few minutes later, arrive at the camp-ground and bergerie at **l'Onda (1385m)**.

V8

	N-S	S-N
Time	3:45	4:30
Distance (km)	7.0	7.0
Ascent (m)	430	887
Descent (m)	887	430
Max Alt (m)	2021	2021

S-N

F **See Map 8.** Take the path to the left of the bergerie at l'Onda. Shortly, TL at a junction and climb steeply. 5min later, pass **Refuge de l'Onda (1431m)**.

4 0:15: TR at a junction beside a big rock: head down the crest of a spur. Soon, TL and descend W off the spur.

3 0:25: From **Bocca d'Oreccia (1427m)**, climb NW close to the crest of a ridge. **See Map 7**. Eventually, reach a gap: use it to cross to the N side of the ridge and then descend steeply. There are sections of scrambling (yellow waymarks). At **Bocca a Meta (1890m)**, climb again.

2 3:00: Reach the summit of **Pointe de Pinzi Corbini (2021m)**. Then keep heading along the ridge. Pass below the summit of Pointe Murace (1921m). Then head N down the ridge.

1 4:00: From **Bocca Manganello (1800m)**, descend N. Then climb across a rocky slope.

S 4:30: Keep SH at a junction to arrive at **Refuge de Petra Piana (1842m)**. The views are spectacular but there is no shade.

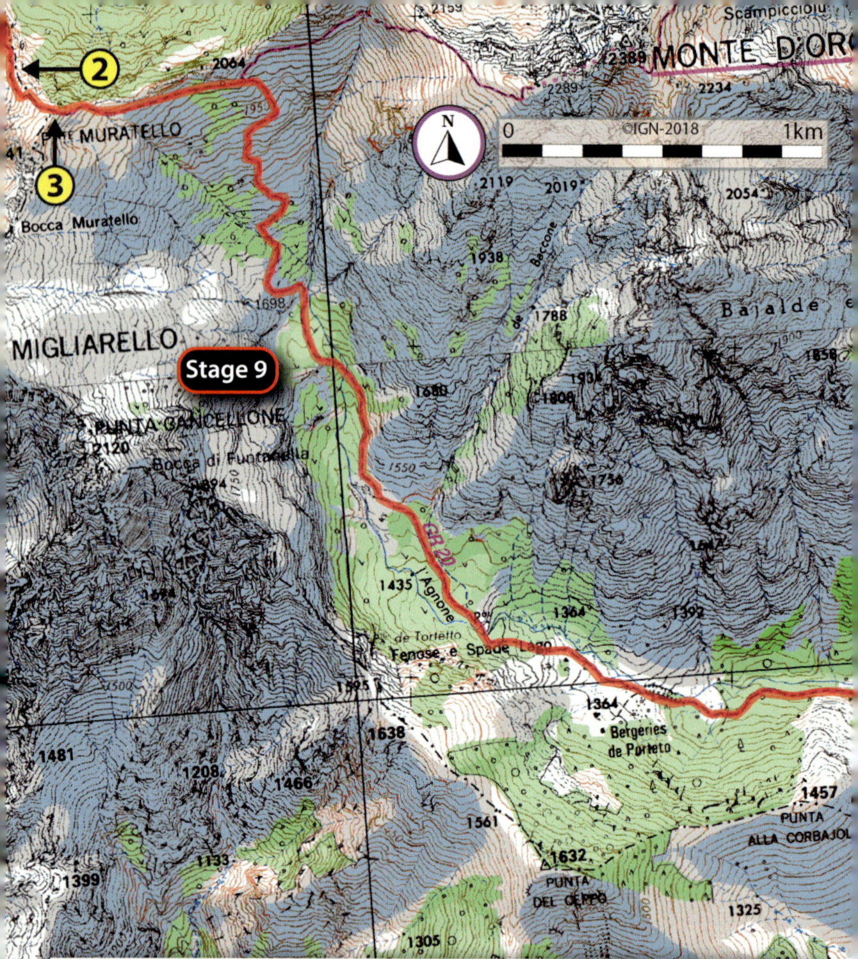

Bags outside the train station in Vizzavona

La Foce Detour

See Map 9. TR at Waypoint No. 5 ('GR20 Sud par Col de Vizzavona'). 15min later, TR onto a road. Shortly afterwards, arrive in **la Foce** where food and accommodation are available. La Foce is 1km from Waypoint No.5.

From la Foce, you can join Stage 10 (close to Bocca Palmente) without having to descend to Vizzavona (3.9km; 1.5hr). Locate the building, on the S side of the road, which is halfway between Hotel Monte d'Oro and Restaurant a Muntagnera: pick up a track to the left of the building ('Sentier de la Femme Perdue').

1. 0:30: TR at a junction onto a track. Soon, ignore a path on the right. TR (uphill) when you meet another track.
2. 1:00: Soon afterwards, TR on a path. **See Map 10.** 10min later, TL at a junction ('Bocca Palmente').
3. 1:30: TR at a junction to join Stage 10.

9

S-N walkers approaching the end of the climb from Vizzavona: note the slabs to be negotiated

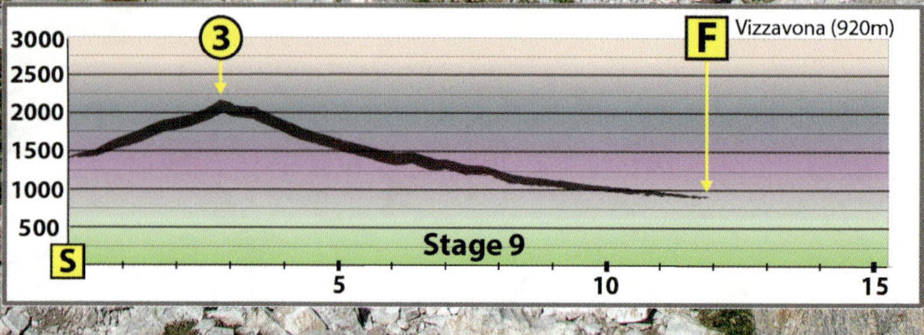

l'Onda to Vizzavona

9

Vizzavona

This is a stage of two halves, both of which are very beautiful. The first section involves a climb up a ridge through grassy terrain to a high pass below Pointe Muratello. Across the pass, the scenery changes dramatically and the second half is a long, knee-jerking descent to Vizzavona through barren rock, shrubs and finally trees. In the forest, the path flanks a stream with plenty of rock-pools for bathing. Many take their time and picnic by the river but others rush on, eager to reach the relative civilisation of Vizzavona.

In places, the climb is steep and rocky. The descent is very long and initially, very steep. Just after Waypoint No.3, there are steep slabs: it would be easy to slip. The waymarks in the forest sections can be hard to follow: the path there is rocky and sometimes unclear.

The tiny village of Vizzavona is an important milestone on the GR20. It is roughly half-way along the trek and it divides the tough northern sections from the easier southern parts. Almost everyone stops there as it offers the best opportunity for resupply on the entire route. The village has a single street where you will find the railway station: beside it there is a restaurant and across the road is the gîte (which also has a bar and a shop). There is also a hotel, another fabulous little shop (beside the train tracks) and a campsite (just W of the centre).

However, many prefer to stay at la Foce which is more peaceful. It is near Col de Vizzavona which is SW of Vizzavona itself: from Waypoint No.5, follow the 'La Foce Detour' (see box). At la Foce, there is accommodation (hotel/gîte/camping) and restaurants. Hotel Monte d'Oro has a shuttle bus for guests who wish to head into Vizzavona.

Water: streams on the descent; la Foce; Vizzavona

Supplies/Meals: Buvette la Cascade (Waypoint No.5); la Foce; Vizzavona

Accommodation: la Foce; Vizzavona

	N-S	S-N
Time	6:00	7:00
Distance (km)	11.9	11.9
Ascent (m)	751	1216
Descent (m)	1216	751
Max Alt (m)	2115	2115

The view N from the pass at Waypoint No.3

N-S

S **See Map 8**. Pick up the path at the left of the bergerie. Shortly, TL at a junction and climb steeply. 5min later, pass **Refuge de l'Onda (1431m)**.

4 0:15: TL at a junction beside a big rock: the path to the right is the variant from Refuge de Petra Piana (Stage v8). Head up the crest of a ridge.

1 0:45: Scramble up some boulders. Soon the gradient increases when the route proceeds over shale.

2 1:55: **See Map 9**. Scramble up a section of steep rocks.

3 2:10: Reach a **pass on the ridge (2115m)**. After viewing the incredible panorama, descend the other side on a clear path. After a few minutes, traverse some steep slabs. Then descend the face of the slabs, following waymarks: watch your footing. At the bottom of the slabs, proceed on a rocky path. Much later, after a stretch through forest, arrive at a pretty plateau. Keep SH following waymarks as the path winds its way down the valley. Enter trees again: shortly after emerging from them, cross a footbridge. 30min later, scramble over some boulders. Afterwards, there are some steep rocky sections which require some scrambling.

4 4:50: TL at a junction ('Gare de Vizzavona'). At times, the waymarks are tricky to follow.

5 5:00: TL at a junction beside a buvette ('la Cascade'), cross a bridge and continue on a good path: alternatively, TR at the junction for the la Foce Detour (see box). 20min later, TR onto another broad path. When you meet a track, TR onto it. A few minutes later, keep SH at a crossroads.

6 5:40: TR onto a rocky path ('Gare de Vizzavona'). Shortly afterwards, cross a bridge. At another junction, TL and cross another bridge. A few minutes later, TL and descend on a small road.

F 6:00: Arrive in **Vizzavona (920m)**.

9

S-N

F **See Map 9**. From Vizzavona, climb SW on the D523. 5-10min later, TR on a path. A few minutes later, cross a bridge and then TR. Shortly afterwards, cross another bridge.

6 0:25: TL onto a track. A few minutes later, keep SH at a crossroads. Shortly afterwards, TL onto a path.

5 1:15: Cross a bridge. Immediately afterwards, TR at a junction beside a buvette ('la Cascade'): the path on the left comes from la Foce (see box: la Foce Detour). Now the waymarks are sometimes tricky to follow.

4 1:25: Keep SH (NW) at a junction. Afterwards, there are some steep rocky sections which require some scrambling. Cross a footbridge and then keep SH following waymarks up the valley. After a while, pass a pretty plateau. Then enter trees again. Eventually, climb across steep slabs: take care.

3 5:30: Cross a **pass on a ridge (2115m)** and descend.

2 5:40: Scramble down a section of steep rocks. Soon there are sections of shale.

1 6:30: **See Map 8**. Scramble down some boulders.

4 6:55: TR at a junction beside a big rock and descend: the path SH is the variant to Refuge de Petra Piana (Stage v8). Soon arrive at **Refuge de l'Onda (1431m)**. Continue downhill to head to the camp-ground.

S 7:00: A few minutes later, arrive at the camp-ground and bergerie at **l'Onda (1385m)**.

10	N-S	S-N
Time	5:30	4:45
Distance (km)	15.0	15.0
Ascent (m)	992	326
Descent (m)	326	992
Max Alt (m)	1641	1641

Vizzavona to Capannelle

10

Gîte u Fugone

The easier southern section of the GR20 begins with a long climb through forest to Bocca Palmente. Here the views open up: the mountain scenery is softer and greener than the rugged rocks of the northern GR20. The undulating traverse around forested slopes which follows is very welcome on a hot day. Later, there is another climb to complete (shorter and steeper than the first), before you begin the short descent to Capannelle.

Navigation is generally straightforward except that on the final descent to Capannelle, the signs/waymarks are confusing. The second climb is steep and can be slippery after rain.

Capannelle can be rather chaotic with a lot of people squeezed into a small space. It is also a confusing place and it is difficult to work out all the accommodation options. At the date of press, there were two places to stay. The GR20 brings you down to Gîte u Fugone (also known as Gîte de Capannelle) which has beds and a camp-ground. The nearby PNRC Refuge d'E Capannelle is situated just above Gîte u Fugone. It is unmanned and cannot be booked on the PNRC website: it is first come, first served and you pay at Gîte u Fugone. At the date of press, Gîte u Renosu (situated on the road above Gîte u Fugone) was closed: if it opens again, you can access it by heading SW along the road after Waypoint No.6 or by climbing W above Gîte u Fugone.

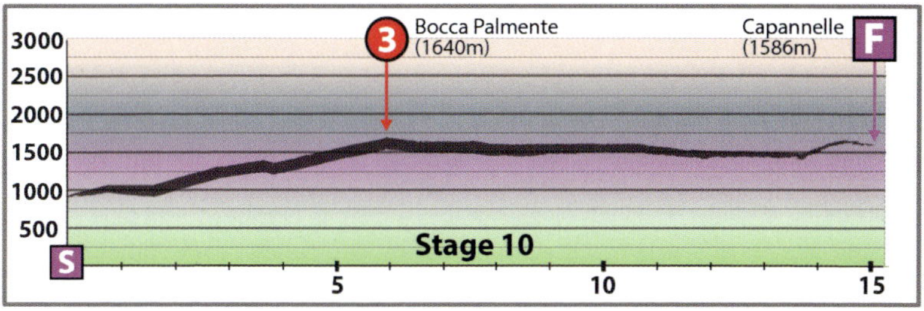

Water: source just W of Bocca Palmente (1600m); streams along the route including those at Bergeries d'Alzeta and Scarpaccedié; source at Gîte u Fugone

Supplies/Meals: Gîte u Fugone; Gîte u Renosu (closed at date of press)

Accommodation: Gîte u Fugone; Gîte u Renosu (closed at date of press); Refuge d'E Capannelle

The view from Bocca Palmente

N-S

S **See Map 9.** From the train station, climb E on a road. Shortly afterwards, TR onto a path (no waymark). 5min later, keep SH at a junction: the waymarks start here. After another 5min, cross a road and continue uphill on a path.

1 0:20: TL on a track. **See Map 10.** At the next junction, TR. A few minutes later, TL onto a path.

2 0:40: TL onto a steep path (easy to miss). 15min later, keep SH at a junction, taking the middle of three paths, continuing uphill.

3 2:40: Cross **Bocca Palmente (1640m)** and descend on a clear path. After 15min, pass the buildings of **Bergeries d'Alzeta (1553m).** The path now makes a long, lovely traverse through forest, undulating gently and offering tantalising glimpses of the peaks between the trees.

4 4:10: Take care fording a stream on large boulders, especially in early season when the water is high.

5 4:30: The path bends sharply left at a junction (easy to miss). 5min later, pass **Bergeries de Scarpaccedié. See Map 11a.** 5-10min later, just after crossing a stream, TR and climb on a steep path which is slippery after rain.

6 5:00: Bear right and climb on a little road. After a few minutes, TL on a path and descend: alternatively, keep SH on the road for Gîte u Renosu.

F 5:30: Arrive at Gîte u Fugone at **Capannelle (1586m).**

10

S-N

F **See Map 11a.** From Gîte u Fugone, head NW on a path: it soon bends right (around the back of the gîte) and climbs. TR onto a small road.

6 0:35: Shortly afterwards, at a hairpin bend, keep SH and descend on a path: it is steep and slippery after rain. TL onto another path. Shortly, cross a stream. 5-10min later, pass **Bergeries de Scarpaccedié**. **See Map 10**.

5 1:00: 5min later, the path bends sharply right at a junction (easy to miss).

4 1:20: Take care fording a stream on large boulders, especially in early season when the water is high. The path now makes a long, lovely traverse through forest, undulating gently and offering tantalising glimpses of the peaks between the trees. Pass the buildings of **Bergeries d'Alzeta (1553m)**.

3 2:50: 20min later, cross **Bocca Palmente (1640m)** and descend on a path.

2 4:15: TR onto a wider path. TR at the next junction. Shortly afterwards, TL onto a track, still descending.

1 4:30: **See Map 9**. Soon TR at a fork. Cross a road and continue N on a path. 5min later, keep SH at a junction: afterwards there are no waymarks. 5min later, TL and descend W on a road.

S 4:45: Shortly afterwards, arrive in **Vizzavona (920m)**.

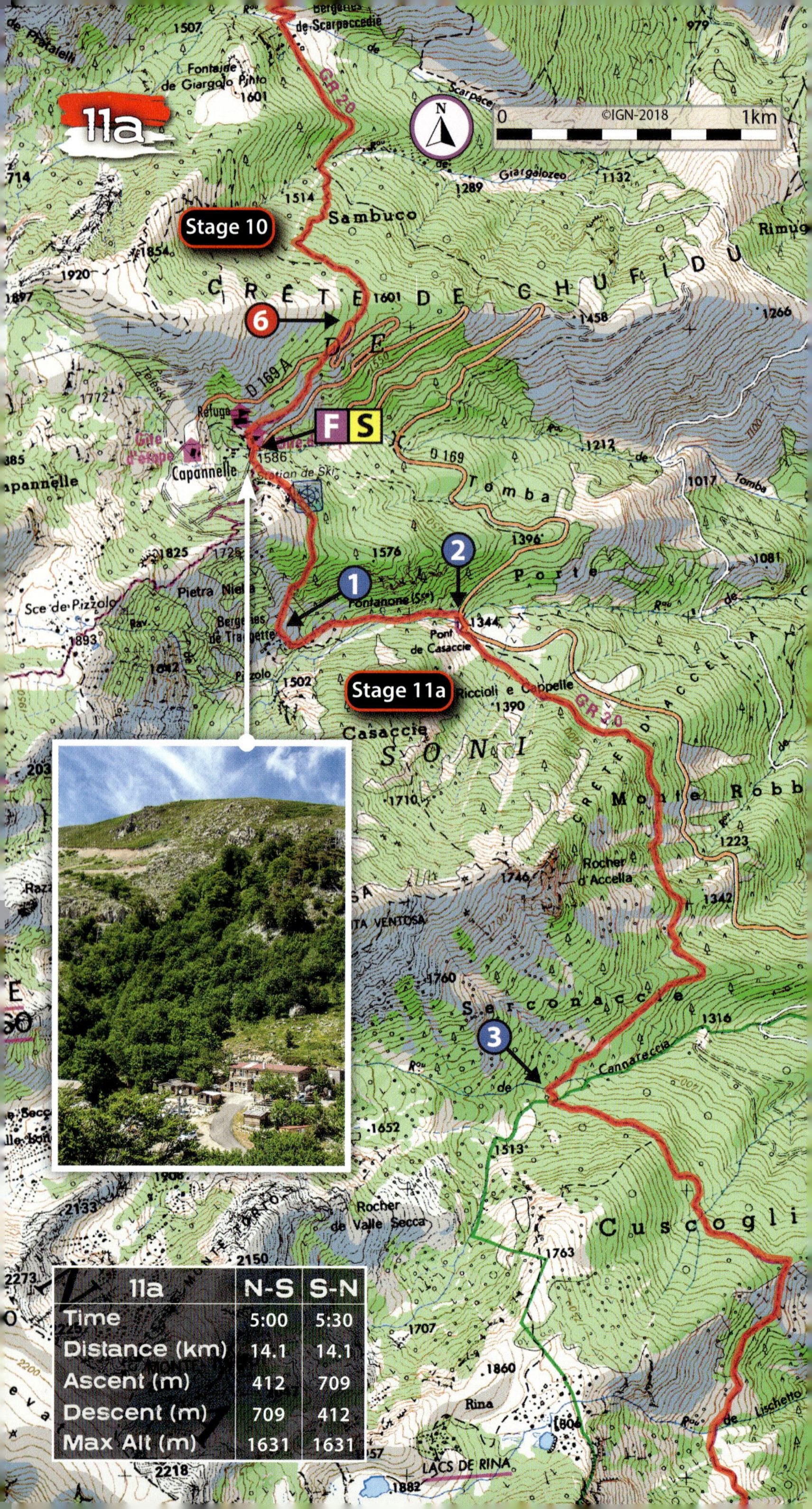

11a	N-S	S-N
Time	5:00	5:30
Distance (km)	14.1	14.1
Ascent (m)	412	709
Descent (m)	709	412
Max Alt (m)	1631	1631

Capannelle to Col de Verde

11a

Rising above the tree-line near Plateau Gialgone

On this stage, the GR20 stays mainly within forests: this is possibly the least scenic part of the trek. It is still a lovely walk though and on the few occasions when you rise above the tree-line, the views are excellent. Look out for Corsican pigs as you approach Col de Verde.

Navigation is straightforward as the stage is well marked. The terrain is undulating but otherwise straightforward.

If you spend the night at Col de Verde, keep your food inside your tent: the pigs have been known to raid trekkers' bags for food at night.

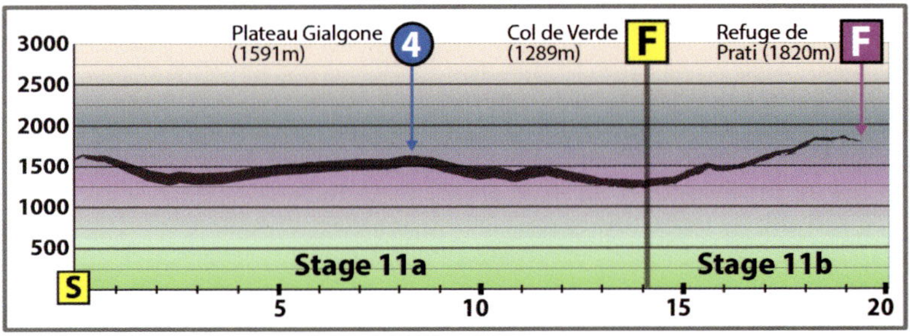

Water: streams along the route; source at Col de Verde

Supplies/Meals: cheese may be available at Bergeries de Traggette; Col de Verde

Accommodation: Relais San Petru di Verde at Col de Verde

11a

N-S

S **See Map 11a**. Head S from Gîte u Fugone, towards a line of pylons. Just after the second pylon, TL on a path. Soon, climb some rocks. Afterwards, descend on a good path.

1 0:40: Pass **Bergeries de Traggette**: some trekkers report that you can bivouac here with the owner's agreement. 15min later, the path passes above a series of waterfalls and rock-pools.

2 1:10: TR onto a road. Shortly afterwards, TR onto a path ('Col de Verde') and head back into forest. For the next 90min, the path climbs in increments. Sometimes there are rocks to clamber over but it is not too difficult.

3 2:10: Ford a pair of torrents on rocks. 20min later, the path finally emerges from the trees: a lovely balcony path contours around the slopes.

4 3:20: **See Map 11b**. The path tops out at **Plateau Gialgone (1591m)**: TL at an area which is almost devoid of vegetation, with one prominent burnt tree trunk. Shortly afterwards, the path starts to descend.

5 4:00: Descend steeply and cross a bridge. Shortly afterwards, proceed down a broad stream bed. Soon, cross the stream bed: take care on the rocks if the water is running. There are salamanders here. A few minutes later, arrive on a broad sandy path.

6 4:55: TL onto a track.

F 5:00: Arrive at **Col de Verde (1289m)**.

S-N

F **See Map 11b**. From Col de Verde, head NW on a track.

6 0:05: TR onto a path. After a while, cross a broad stream bed: take care on the rocks if the water is running. There are salamanders here. Then proceed up the stream bed.

5 1:00: Shortly afterwards, cross a bridge. Then climb steeply.

4 2:10: After a long climb, TR at an area which is almost devoid of vegetation. Shortly afterwards, the path tops out at **Plateau Gialgone (1591m)**. Afterwards, a lovely balcony path contours around the slopes (generally losing altitude).

3 3:10: **See Map 11a**. Ford a pair of torrents on rocks. Now the path descends through the forest in increments. Sometimes there are rocks to clamber over but it is not too difficult. Eventually, TL onto a road.

2 4:00: Shortly afterwards, TL onto a path and climb: the path passes above a series of waterfalls and rock pools.

1 4:45: Pass **Bergeries de Traggette**: some trekkers report that you can bivouac here with the owner's agreement. Afterwards, climb on a good path. Soon, descend over rocks.

S 5:30: TR onto a track and just afterwards, arrive at Gîte u Fugone at **Capannelle (1586m)**.

Col de Verde to Refuge de Prati

11b

The climb to Bocca d'Oru

After the forest walk on Stage 11a, you emerge from the trees. The scenery is the finest so far on the southern section of the GR20. Climb through forest at the start of the stage: it is steep and/or rocky in places but never too difficult. There are tantalising mountain views between the trees and when you rise above the tree-line, the vista is wonderful.

Finally a magnificent traverse through a grassy plateau brings you to one of the loveliest refuges on the trek: Refuge de Prati has stunning views of the neighbouring peaks and the Mediterranean Sea. There are some fabulous grassy camping pitches. Navigation is straightforward.

Water: source at Refuge de Prati

Supplies/Meals: Refuge de Prati

Accommodation: Refuge de Prati

0
©IGN-2018
1km
GR 20
Stage 11a
Col de la Flasca
Pont de Marmano
Marmano
Gialgone
CRETE DE PIETRA SCOPINA
4
5
6
GR 20
CINTELLO DELLA MONDA

Salamander

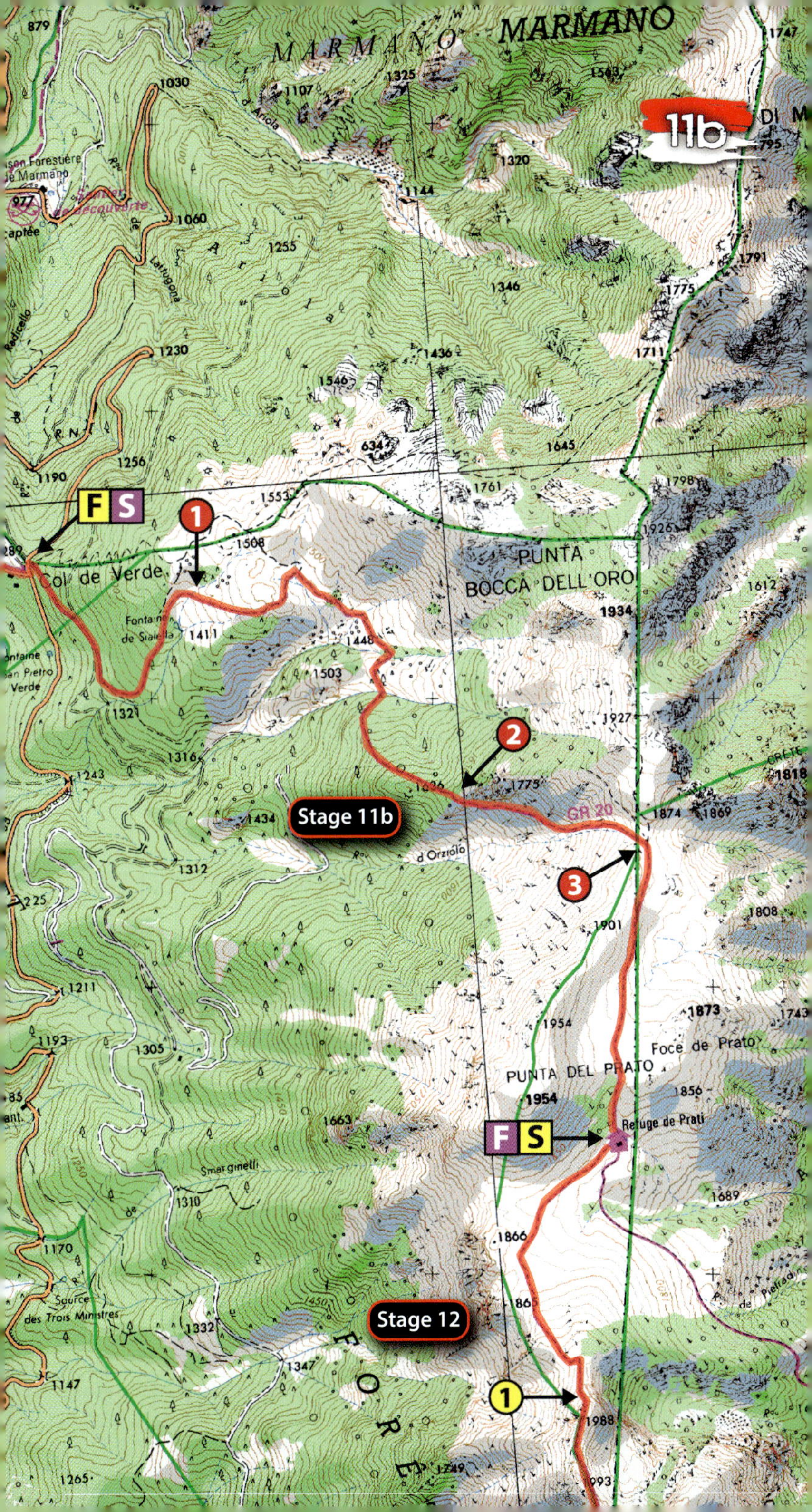
11b
MARMANO
Stage 11b
Stage 12
Col de Verde
PUNTA BOCCA DELL'ORO
PUNTA DEL PRATO
Foce de Prato
Refuge de Prati
GR 20
F S

	N-S	S-N
Time	2:15	1:45
Distance (km)	5.1	5.1
Ascent (m)	587	56
Descent (m)	56	587
Max Alt (m)	1856	1856

N-S

S **See Map 11b**. From the refuge at Col de Verde, TR and climb briefly to a road: cross over and pick up a path. 10min later, keep SH across a junction, still climbing. When the path bends left, the gradient increases substantially. 5min later, TL at a fork. Now simply follow waymarks up through the trees.

1 0:35: Rise above the tree-line and arrive at a plateau. Shortly, enter trees again. Soon afterwards, start to climb steeply.

2 1:15: Emerge from the trees again: now the path climbs through rock outcrops.

3 1:55: Keep SH across **Bocca d'Oru (1840m)** and follow a clear path across a wonderful grassy plateau.

F 2:15: Arrive at **Refuge de Prati (1820m)**.

Refuge de Prati is set on a beautiful plateau

11b

S-N

F **See Map 11b**. From Refuge de Prati, climb N on a path. Soon, the route levels and heads across a wonderful grassy plateau.

3 0:20: Cross **Bocca d'Oru (1840m)** and descend W through rock outcrops.

2 0:45: Enter trees, still descending.

1 1:20: Cross a plateau. Afterwards, simply follow waymarks down through the trees: ignore offshoots. After a while, TL at a fork.

S 1:45: Shortly afterwards, TL on a road to arrive at **Col de Verde (1289m)** where you will find the refuge known as Relais San Petru di Verde.

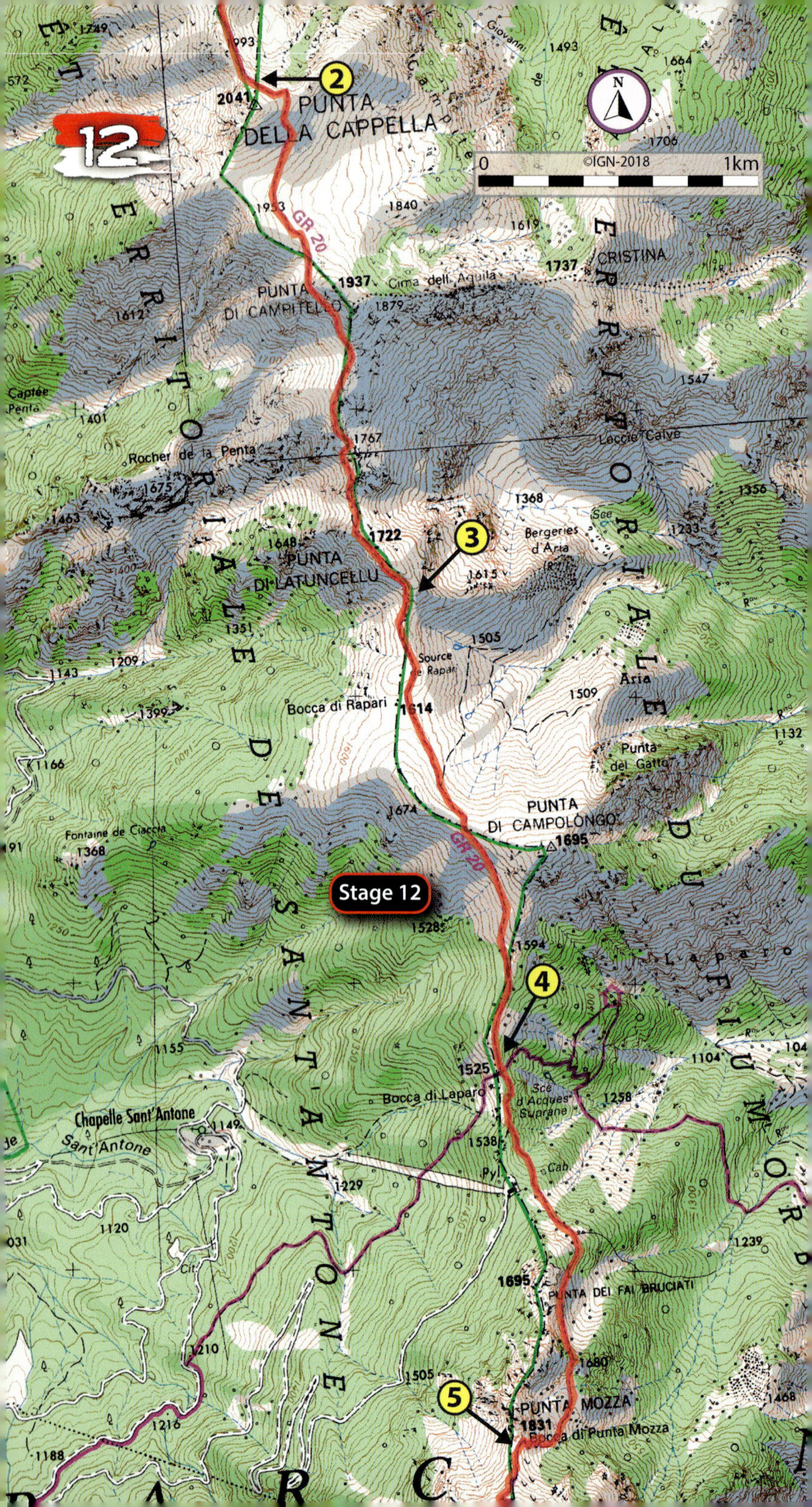
12
PUNTA DELLA CAPPELLA
2041
GR 20
PUNTA DI CAMPITELLO
1937
Cima dell' Aquila
CRISTINA
1737
Rocher de la Penta
1767
PUNTA DI LATUNCELLU
1722
Bergeries d'Aria
Source de Rapari
Bocca di Rapari
1614
Aria
Punta del Gatto
PUNTA DI CAMPOLONGO
1695
Fontaine de Ciaccia
Stage 12
Bocca di Laparo
1525
Chapelle Sant'Antone
Sant'Antone
PUNTA DEI FAI BRUCIATI
PUNTA MOZZA
1831
Bocca di Punta Mozza
TERRITORIALE DE SANT'ANTONE
TERRITORIALE DU FIUMORBO
©IGN-2018
0
1km
N

Refuge de Prati to Refuge d'Usciolu

12

One of the joys of the GR20 is its ability to show-off so many different types of scenery and Stage 12 is completely unlike what has come before. For the most part, it is a wonderful ridge walk and the views are incredible throughout. However, the terrain changes constantly: the path winds its way along, close to the crest, sometimes through beautiful grassy plateaus and sometimes amongst jagged rock outcrops. If we had to pick only one stage of the southern half of the GR20, then this would be it.

The camping pitches at Refuge d'Usciolu are fabulous: there are many little flat areas amongst the rocks with spectacular views to the S. The shop at the refuge is normally very well stocked. Be sure to pay your camping fee before you go to bed.

The route undulates throughout and is therefore tiring. Often there is a good, clear path but at other times, you will scramble over boulders. In good conditions, navigation is straightforward. However, in bad weather or low visibility, the waymarks are sometimes hard to follow.

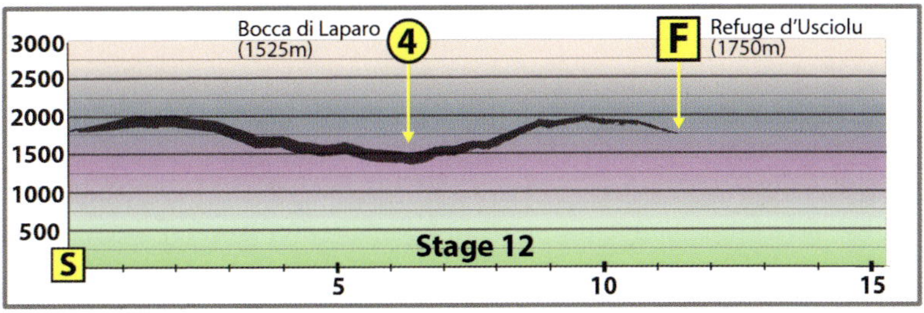

Water: source near Bocca di Laparo (often dry); source at Refuge d'Usciolu

Supplies/Meals: Refuge d'Usciolu

Accommodation: Refuge d'Usciolu

The amazing view from Refuge d'Usciolu

	N-S	S-N
Time	5:45	6:00
Distance (km)	11.3	11.3
Ascent (m)	773	843
Descent (m)	843	773
Max Alt (m)	1981	1981

N-S

S **See Map 11b**. Head SW on a clear path. After 10min, the path bends left and climbs towards some outcrops.

1 0:35: Scramble up rocks to reach a ridge: continue close to the crest. A few minutes later, cross another section of rocks: some scrambling is required. Soon, drop to the left side of the ridge: take care to follow the waymarks, especially in low visibility.

2 1:05: **See Map 12**. Cross a little col just underneath Punta della Cappella and descend. 45min later, cross a section of boulders (no path).

3 2:25: Enter trees and enjoy some shade. 15min later, cross **Bocca di Rapari (1614m)**, a beautiful zone of grass and deciduous trees.

4 3:10: Arrive at **Bocca di Laparo (1525m)**: there is an information board identifying the neighbouring peaks. Keep SH ('Usciolu'), heading S. Afterwards, the path undulates but gradually works its way upwards. After a while, the gradient increases: this is the start of a long, steep climb.

5 4:25: Cross the beautiful **Bocca di Punta Mozza (1800m)**. Shortly afterwards, descend briefly and then climb again. **See Map 13a**. Soon, scramble up boulders for 5-10min to reach the summit of **Punta Bianca (1954m)**. Descend SW, following waymarks across rocks. Shortly, pick up a path. Take care descending some slabs. Shortly afterwards, TR and climb over slabs back to the crest of the ridge: do not drop to the left where there is a clear path. Follow waymarks along the crest.

6 5:15: Arrive at the summit of **Monte Furmicula (1981m)**. Soon afterwards, start to descend.

F 5:45: Arrive at **Refuge d'Usciolu (1750m)**.

12

S-N

F **See Map 13a.** From Refuge d'Usciolu, climb NE on a path.

6 0:45: Arrive at the summit of **Monte Furmicula (1981m)**. Follow waymarks along the crest: do not drop to the right where there is a clear path. Climb down some slabs and then TL. Shortly afterwards, descend some more slabs. Soon climb NE, following waymarks across rocks to reach the summit of **Punta Bianca (1954m)**. Then scramble down some boulders.

5 1:40: **See Map 12.** Climb briefly and cross the beautiful **Bocca di Punta Mozza (1800m)**. Afterwards, begin a long, steep descent. Then the path undulates but gradually works its way downwards.

4 2:40: Arrive at **Bocca di Laparo (1525m)**: there is an information board identifying the neighbouring peaks. Keep SH, heading N. After a while, cross **Bocca di Rapari (1614m)**, a beautiful zone of grass and deciduous trees.

3 3:40: 20min later, enter trees and enjoy some shade. After a while, cross a section of boulders (no path).

2 5:10: Climb over a little col just underneath Punta della Cappella and descend. **See Map 11b.** Soon, drop to the right side of the ridge: take care to follow the waymarks, especially in low visibility. Cross another section of rocks: some scrambling is required.

1 5:40: Climb up to the crest of the ridge again. Then scramble down some rocks. Afterwards, a path descends to a plateau and then bends right.

S 6:00: Arrive at **Refuge de Prati (1820m)**.

13a
PARC
MONTE FURMICULA
Stage 12
6
Crête d'Acqua d'Acelli
Bocca di Suragheddu
Refuge d'Usciolu
Cozzano Escape
F
S
Fontaine du Pantaneddu
Bocca di l'Usciolu
Stage 13a
Punta di l'Usciolu
GR 20
a Rughia
PUNTA BIA
Collu di F
©IGN-2018
0
1km
Bergeries de Basseta (1315m)
Refuge de Matalza (1410m)
3000
2500
2000
1500
1000
500
Stage 13a
Stage 13b
5
10
15

Refuge d'Usciolu to Bergeries de Basseta

13a

Sunrise is a lovely time on the ridge

Climb briefly onto the ridge just to the W of Refuge d'Usciolu. As the path winds in and out of outcrops along the crest, the views are sublime: it is particularly fabulous in the early morning light when the sun hits the unusual rock formations. Eventually, when you descend and leave the ridge behind, the scenery changes dramatically: you enter a fertile zone of pastures and trees which is quite unlike anything that you have seen so far. Although you are still some days from the end of the trek, there is a clear sense of change: you are leaving the highest mountains behind and your journey will soon draw to a close. Many people cool down in the lovely rock-pools at Waypoint No.4.

Bergeries de Basseta is the most northerly of three bergeries which offer food and accommodation. It is well supplied and the restaurant is good. As well as tent pitches, there are chalets for 4-6 people and a dormitory.

Along the ridge, the terrain is rocky and there is some scrambling: follow waymarks carefully. Otherwise, the path is clear and simple to follow.

Water: river at Waypoint No.4; Bergeries de Basseta

Supplies/Meals: Bergeries de Basseta

Accommodation: Bergeries de Basseta

Escape/Access: from Bocca di Suragheddu, a path descends to Cozzano: see 'Cozzano Escape' below. The descent is long, dropping almost 1100m. From Cozzano, Sud Cars runs a bus service to Ajaccio: +33 (0)4 95 73 27 44. The bus runs daily in July/August but during the rest of the year, there is no Sunday service. In Cozzano, there are a few restaurants and places to stay.

From Waypoint No.3, a path descends to Zicavo: see 'Zicavo Escape A' below. The altitude loss is around 700m. From Zicavo, Sud Cars (see above) runs buses to Ajaccio. The bus runs daily in July/August but during the rest of the year, there is no Sunday service. Alternatively, Taxi VTC (based in Zicavo; +33 (0)6 41 24 15 00) can take you to various Corsican destinations: it can pick up/drop off at some GR20 refuges/bergeries.

In Zicavo, there are a few restaurants, a shop and some places to stay. If walking N-S, you could also use Zicavo Escape A to resupply in Zicavo (perhaps with an overnight stay) and then follow Zicavo Escape B (see Stage 13b) to return to the GR20.

13a

	N-S	S-N
Time	3:45	4:30
Distance (km)	9.6	9.6
Ascent (m)	301	736
Descent (m)	736	301
Max Alt (m)	1834	1834

The route along the ridge involves some scrambling

N-S

S **See Map 13a**. Climb SW. 5-10min later, TL at **Bocca di Suragheddu (1805m)**: alternatively keep SH for the **Cozzano Escape** (see below). Follow waymarks along the crest of a ridge: there is some scrambling. Watch out for a huge rock where the path appears to run steeply down to the left: instead loop around the right side of the rock for a safer descent.

1 1:55: **See Map 13b**. The big descent of the stage begins. There is a steep section over boulders but soon, the gradient eases and you enter trees.

2 2:20: TR at a junction at **Bocca di l'Agnone (1570m)**: alternatively, TL for the **Asinau Direct Route** (see below). 25min later, emerge from the trees and enter a fertile zone of grassy pastures.

3 3:00: Keep SH at a junction: alternatively, TR for **Zicavo Escape A**.

4 3:20: Cross a river with some beautiful rock-pools. Afterwards, the path proceeds delightfully alongside the river. Soon, the route bends right (away from the river) and climbs. 5min later, cross a track and pick up a path on the other side (easy to miss).

F 3:45: Arrive at **Bergeries de Basseta (1315m)**.

Cozzano Escape

5.1km/2.75hr from Refuge d'Usciolu to Cozzano; yellow and orange waymarks; see Map 13a.

From Bocca di Suragheddu, descend SW on a well-marked path ('Cozzano'). After a while, pass a source (Fontaine de Pantaneddu) where you can normally fill your bottles. TL onto a track. A few hundred metres later, TR on a path. Eventually, cross another track and pick up another path (orange waymarks): as it descends, the path soon cuts across a number of hairpins in the track. TL onto the D69 to enter Cozzano (727m): alternatively TR to go to the gîte.

S-N

F **See Map 13b**. The GR20 heads NE past Bergeries de Basseta and then bends to the N. After a while, cross a track and pick up a path on the other side. Descend and soon the route bends left to follow the river.

4 0:30: Cross a river with some beautiful rock-pools. Afterwards, climb.

3 1:00: Keep SH at a junction, climbing: alternatively, TL for **Zicavo Escape A**.

2 2:00: TL at a junction at **Bocca di l'Agnone (1570m)**, still climbing: the path on the right is the **Asinau Direct Route** (see below). After leaving the trees, there is a steep section over boulders.

1 2:45: Arrive near the crest of the ridge: follow waymarks NE along it. There are sections of scrambling. **See Map 13a**. Eventually, TR at **Bocca di Suragheddu (1805m)** and descend off the ridge: alternatively TL for the **Cozzano Escape** (see below).

S 4:30: 5min later, arrive at **Refuge d'Usciolu (1750m)**.

The view from the ridge at sunrise

Asinau Direct Route

16.1km/7hr from Refuge d'Usciolu to Refuge d'Asinau; yellow waymarks

You can avoid Stages 13b, 14a and most of 14b by leaving Stage 13a at Waypoint No.2 on a variant route which takes you more directly to Refuge d'Asinau. This lovely but challenging route makes for a long day but it has the advantage of passing over the summit of Monte Alcudina. Some scrambling is required.

See Map 13b. From Waypoint No.2, head E. After 1hr, keep SH across a track on a path. Soon afterwards, TL descending E. Cross a bridge over a stream. **See Map 14a**. Soon pass the ruins of Refuge Pedinielli (1623m): you are permitted to camp here. Keep climbing and shortly, pass a water source. When you reach a bocca on a ridge (Crête de la Foce Aperta), TR and climb S up the crest of the ridge. After a while, the route passes along the right side of the ridge. Pass over the summit of Monte Alcudina (2134m) and then descend SW along the crest of the ridge. When you arrive at Waypoint No.3 of Stage 14b, TL and descend to Refuge d'Asinau.

Zicavo Escape A

4.9km/2hr from Waypoint No.3 to Zicavo; yellow and orange waymarks

See Map 13b. Head NW from Waypoint No.3. Soon descend through trees. TR onto a track. A few minutes later, TR and descend on a path. TL at a junction of paths. Follow waymarks all the way to the D69. Then TL to enter Zicavo (721m).

Bergeries de Basseta to Refuge de Matalza

13b

Refuge de Matalza

It is a short, pretty walk to Refuge de Matalza. You may be glad of the shade provided by the many trees. Navigation and terrain are straightforward.

Although the refuge has a more beautiful setting than Bergeries de Basseta, the facilities are not quite as good.

N-S

S **See Map 13b**. The GR20 continues at the S side of Bergeries de Basseta.

1 0:20: Keep SH at a junction of paths: alternatively, TR for Zicavo Escape B (see below). Shortly afterwards, on arrival at a road, keep SH, passing to the right of **Chapelle San Petru**. Soon, start to climb through forest. 10min later, TR along a gravel lane.

F 0:45: Arrive at **Refuge de Matalza (1410m)**.

S-N

F **See Map 13b**. From Refuge de Matalza, head NW on a track. 5min later, TL onto a path. Follow waymarks down through forest. Keep SH, passing to the left of **Chapelle San Petru**. Shortly afterwards, keep SH across a road, continuing on a path.

1 0:15: Keep SH at a junction of paths: alternatively, TL for Zicavo Escape B.

S 0:30: Arrive at **Bergeries de Basseta (1315m)**.

Water: source at San Petru; Refuge de Matalza

Supplies/Meals: Refuge de Matalza

Accommodation: you may be able to sleep on the floor of the old refuge at San Petru (no facilities); Refuge de Matalza

Escape/Access: from Waypoint No.1, a straightforward path descends through forest to Zicavo: see 'Zicavo Escape B' below. The altitude loss is around 650m. From Zicavo, Sud Cars runs a bus service to Ajaccio: see Stage 13a for further information on the bus and Zicavo. Alternatively, Taxi VTC (based in Zicavo; +33 (0)6 41 24 15 00) can take you to various Corsican destinations: it can pick up/drop off at some GR20 refuges/bergeries If walking S-N, you could also use Zicavo Escape B to resupply in Zicavo (perhaps with an overnight stay) and then follow Zicavo Escape A (see Stage 13a) to return to the GR20.

13b	N-S	S-N
Time	0:45	0:30
Distance (km)	2.0	2.0
Ascent (m)	105	10
Descent (m)	10	105
Max Alt (m)	1410	1410

Zicavo Escape B

5.8km/2hr from blue Waypoint No.1 to Zicavo; yellow waymarks

Head W from Waypoint No.1. Soon TL onto the D428. Shortly afterwards, TR at a monument and descend NW on a path through trees. Eventually, TR onto the D69 and follow it to Zicavo (721m).

Refuge de Matalza to Bergerie de Croci

14a

Bergerie de Croci

This short but beautiful stage involves a climb alongside the cool waters of the Ruisseau de Croce, through soft, rolling terrain of grass and trees. It is not as dramatic as some other parts of the trek but it is wonderful nonetheless. Furthermore, it provides one of the rare opportunities for relaxation on the GR20: take it slowly and enjoy! The path is easy to follow and well marked.

N-S

S **See Map 13b**. Head SE along the track in front of the refuge. 5min later, TR at a fork. A few minutes later, TR at another fork, continuing alongside the river.

1 0:35: **See Map 14a**. TR at another fork onto a narrow path.

F 1:00: Arrive at **Bergerie de Croci (1543m)** with its grassy camp-ground overlooking the mountains.

S-N

F From Bergerie de Croci, descend N on a path.

1 0:20: Keep SH at a junction. Soon the path bends right and follows the river N: at any junctions, keep close to the river. Shortly after crossing a bridge, TL at a junction.

S 0:45: 5min later, arrive at **Refuge de Matalza (1410m)**.

Water: streams; Bergerie de Croci

Supplies/Meals: Bergerie de Croci

Accommodation: Bergerie de Croci

14a	N-S	S-N
Time	1:00	0:45
Distance (km)	3.1	3.1
Ascent (m)	155	15
Descent (m)	15	155
Max Alt (m)	1550	1550

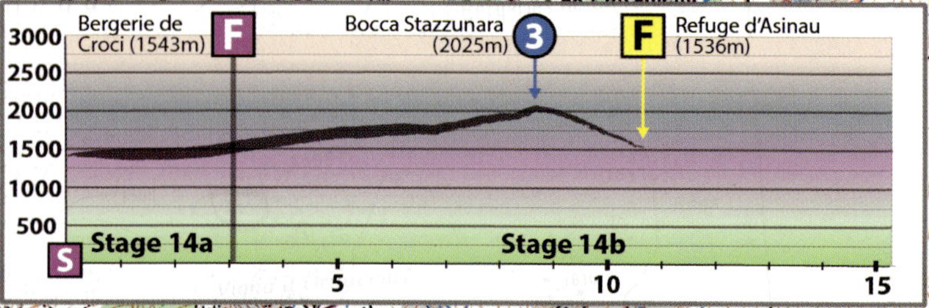

14a
Asinau Direct Route
GR 20 variante
Pedinielli Refuge ruiné
Pedinielli Berg. rnee
1623
1601
1695
Pargolu
1606
1833
Foce
1817
1843
1805
Col de Luana
Crête de la Foce
1844
1513
1638
1762
©IGN-2018
0
1km
2014
2033
Bocca d'a R
Pilier
Punta Scarachiana
2126
Punta di Valli Tremuli
2129
Calv.
2134
MONTE ALCUDINA (MONTE INCUDINE)
1731
Crête de Concatellu
1836
2025
1881
1637
Ritondu
2046
GR 20
2007
Funtana
F
S
Refuge d'
1536
Bergeries d'Asinau
1386
de Menta
Stage 15
Ravin
Fne de Partusu
Liaison
1881
Longa
1875
1239
Fne d'Alzitella

14b

The trail snaking across pastures near Bergerie de Croci

Bergerie de Croci to Refuge d'Asinau

14b

Wonderfully green terrain on the way to Bocca Stazzunara

Start with a glorious journey through rolling hills, climbing gently. Later the gradient increases and you top-out at Bocca Stazzunara: this is the last time the GR20 rises above 2000m. The views are sublime at the pass but, for an even better panorama, many climb (off-route) to the nearby summit of Monte Alcudina. Finally, a steep and difficult descent leads to the beautifully situated Refuge d'Asinau.

Avoid this stage in low visibility or bad weather. The descent from Bocca Stazzunara to Refuge d'Asinau is one of the most challenging sections of the entire GR20 and would be hazardous in wet conditions: there are steep slabs of granite to cross and a fall would be serious. There are also large boulders to scramble down. Follow waymarks carefully as you descend.

Water: Refuge d'Asinau

Supplies/Meals: Refuge d'Asinau

Accommodation: Refuge d'Asinau

14b

	N-S	S-N
Time	3:30	3:30
Distance (km)	7.5	7.5
Ascent (m)	488	502
Descent (m)	502	488
Max Alt (m)	2025	2025

The view S from Bocca Stazzunara

N-S

S **See Map 14a**. Climb S on a path. A few minutes later, TR up a track.

1 0:20: TL onto a path and climb steeply up some slabs. A few minutes later, continue upwards on a clear path. Soon, TR onto a rough track. Shortly afterwards, TL and climb on a path.

2 1:30: TR and leave the path, heading straight up the slope (cairns/waymarks): this junction is easy to miss. The gradient gets steeper as you progress and there are some rocks to scramble over.

3 2:20: Arrive at **Bocca Stazzunara (2025m)**: TL if you wish to climb to the summit of Monte Alcudina. Otherwise, keep SH over the bocca and descend steeply. Take great care on sheer slabs. Occasionally, you must climb briefly before descending again.

F 3:30: Arrive at **Refuge d'Asinau (1536m)**.

S-N

F **See Map 14a**. From Refuge d'Asinau, climb W on a path. Soon the route bends right, climbing more steeply (NW). The higher you get, the more difficult the climb becomes: there is some scrambling. Towards the top, take care climbing sheer slabs.

3 1:40: Arrive at **Bocca Stazzunara (2025m)**: TR if you wish to climb to the summit of Monte Alcudina. Otherwise, keep SH over the bocca and descend W. There are some rocks to scramble down (cairns/waymarks).

2 2:15: TL onto another path and start to contour around the slopes: keep on the main path, ignoring offshoots. Soon the path heads N. After a while, TL at a fork to descend NW. TR onto a track. Just afterwards, TL on a path. Shortly, TR at a faint junction.

1 3:15: A few minutes later, climb down some steep slabs. Then TR and descend on a track.

S 3:30: Arrive at **Bergerie de Croci (1543m)** with its grassy camp-ground overlooking the mountains.

Refuge d'Asinau to Village de Bavella

15

Col de Bavella

An undulating trip through the forested slopes below the Aiguilles de Bavella. Much of your time will be spent amongst the trees but, when you do emerge from them, the scenery is magnificent: the vantage points overlooking the spires of the famous Aiguilles are superb. Finally, there is a steep, rocky climb to Col de Bavella: on a hot day it will be a relief to enter the nearby village of Bavella, where you can relax with a cool drink.

This stage is quite tiring because the route undulates constantly. The altitude gain and loss are greater than they would appear on paper. The relatively low altitude means that this area can be very hot but fortunately there is shade amongst the many trees. The rocks and roots in the forest are slippery after rain. The final climb to Col de Bavella is rocky and steep. The waymarks are occasionally hard to follow.

Stage 15 is often over-shadowed by the more dramatic 'Alpine Variant' (Stage v15) which takes you right up to the Aiguilles.

Water: streams before Waypoint No.1; fountain in Bavella village opposite the gîte

Supplies/Meals: Col de Bavella; Bavella

Accommodation: Col de Bavella; Bavella

Escape/Access: in July/August, there is usually a daily bus service between Bavella, Propriano and Ajaccio: at the date of press, it was not clear which business would operate the service in 2024 and beyond. In July/August, Balesi Evasion runs daily bus services from Bavella to Porto-Vecchio and Ajaccio: www.balesievasion.com; +33 (0)6 12 85 67 66/(0)4 95 70 02 50

15	N-S	S-N
Time	5:00	5:30
Distance (km)	12.0	12.0
Ascent (m)	422	775
Descent (m)	775	422
Max Alt (m)	1536	1536

The forest terrain on Stage 15

N-S

S **See Map 14a**. Head SW on a path. 20min later, keep SH at a junction and descend on a path into forest: it is tiring crossing rocks and tree roots. After descending for 20min, the path climbs through the forest. After 10-15min of climbing, the path levels. **See Map 15**. Soon, start to descend gently again. When the gradient gets steeper, take care to follow waymarks as the path is easy to lose. Shortly afterwards, cross a stream, climbing briefly on the other side. Soon, descend gently.

1 1:15: Keep SH at a junction: alternatively, TL for Stage v15. The path now undulates relentlessly through the trees, gradually making its way downwards.

2 2:45: Keep SH at a junction.

3 4:00: Start the final ascent which is steep and tiring: there are some sections of boulders.

4 4:45: Keep SH at a junction: this is where Stage v15 rejoins the main GR20.

5 4:55: Arrive at **Col de Bavella (1218m)**: TL and walk down a road. Continue past Gîte les Aiguilles de Bavella which has a restaurant.

F 5:00: A few minutes later, arrive at **Village de Bavella (1180m)** which has a gîte, restaurant, sandwich bar and shop.

S-N

F **See Map 15**. From Bavella, climb NW on a road. Continue past Gîte les Aiguilles de Bavella which has a restaurant.

5 0:10: At **Col de Bavella (1218m)**, TR on a path.

4 0:15: TL at a junction: alternatively TR for Stage v15. Continue descending, often steeply: there are some sections of boulders.

2 1:45: Keep SH at a junction. The path now undulates relentlessly through the trees, gradually making its way upwards.

1 3:45: Keep SH at a junction: this is where Stage v15 rejoins the main GR20. Climb gently. Then descend, cross a stream and climb on the other side: take care to follow waymarks as the path is easy to lose. **See Map 14a**. Shortly after the path levels, descend again. Soon climb more steeply: it is tiring crossing rocks and tree roots. Keep SH at a junction and continue climbing.

S 5:30: Arrive at **Refuge d'Asinau (1536m)**.

v15

Expansive views from the Aiguilles de Bavella

N-S

S **See Map 14a**. Head SW on a path. 20min later, keep SH at a junction and descend into forest: it is tiring crossing rocks/tree roots. After descending for 20min, climb through the forest: after 10-15min of climbing, the path levels. **See Map 15**. Soon, descend gently again. When the gradient gets steeper, take care to follow waymarks as the path is easy to lose. Shortly afterwards, cross a stream, climbing briefly on the other side. Soon, descend gently.

1 1:15: TL at a junction ('Alpine Variant'): alternatively, keep SH for Stage 15. Climb steeply SE, following yellow waymarks. Pass underneath **Punta Longa (Tower 5)** and head S towards **Punta di u Pargulu (Tower 4)**.

2 2:15: Cross **Bocca di u Pargulu (1662m)** and descend. Pass below **Punta di a Vacca (Tower 3)**. Then follow the rocky path towards a bocca between Tower 3 and **Punta di l'Arjettu (Tower 2)**. Pass underneath Tower 2.

3 3:10: Climb up to the foot of a steep slab. Then use fixed chains to scale the slab: take great care. Afterwards, descend and then climb to a gap. Now, descend steeply through a rocky gully: watch out for rock-falls.

4 4:00: TL at a junction: this is where Stage v15 rejoins the main GR20.

5 4:10: Arrive at **Col de Bavella (1218m)**: TL and walk down a road. Continue past Gîte les Aiguilles de Bavella which has a restaurant.

F 4:15: A few minutes later, arrive at **Village de Bavella (1180m)** which has a gîte, restaurant, sandwich bar and shop.

S-N

F **See Map 15**. From Bavella, climb NW on a road. Continue past Gîte les Aiguilles de Bavella which has a restaurant.

5 0:05: At **Col de Bavella (1218m)**, TR on a path.

4 0:10: TR at a junction: alternatively TL for Stage 15. Start to climb steeply: soon head up a rocky gully. Watch out for rock-falls. Cross a gap and then descend. Soon climb again.

3 1:40: Use fixed chains to climb down a steep slab: take great care. Pass underneath **Punta di l'Arjettu (Tower 2)**. Follow the rocky path towards a bocca between Tower 2 and **Punta di a Vacca (Tower 3)**. Pass below Tower 3. Then climb again.

2 2:30: Cross **Bocca di u Pargulu (1662m)** and head N. Pass underneath **Punta Longa (Tower 5)**. Soon, descend steeply NW (yellow waymarks).

1 3:00: TR at a junction: this is where Stage v15 rejoins Stage 15. Climb gently. Then descend, cross a stream and climb on the other side: take care to follow waymarks as the path is easy to lose. **See Map 14a**. Shortly after the path levels, descend again. Soon climb more steeply: it is tiring crossing rocks and tree roots. Keep SH at a junction and continue climbing.

S 4:45: Arrive at **Refuge d'Asinau (1536m)**.

Refuge d'Asinau to Village de Bavella (Alpine Variant)

v15

The Aiguilles de Bavella

On Stage 15 there are beautiful views of the Aiguilles de Bavella, seen from afar. However, Stage v15 brings you much closer to them. This 'Alpine Variant' also travels higher altitudes so the views are more expansive.

	N-S	S-N
Time	4:15	4:45
Distance (km)	7.7	7.7
Ascent (m)	590	946
Descent (m)	946	590
Max Alt (m)	1660	1660

The terrain is challenging: often steep, rocky and exposed. There are sections of scrambling. At Waypoint No.3, there is a difficult slab to climb with a fixed chain to assist: take great care as a fall would be serious. The slab is treacherous when wet. This stage is not suitable for those with a fear of heights. Follow waymarks closely to avoid getting lost: navigation would be tricky in poor conditions. Avoid this stage in low visibility, bad weather or after rain.

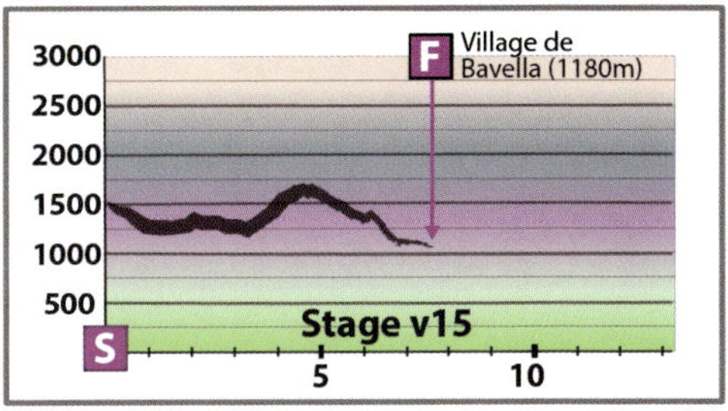

Water: streams before Waypoint No.1; fountain in Bavella village opposite the gîte

Supplies/Meals: Col de Bavella; Bavella

Accommodation: Col de Bavella; Bavella

Escape/Access: see Stage 15

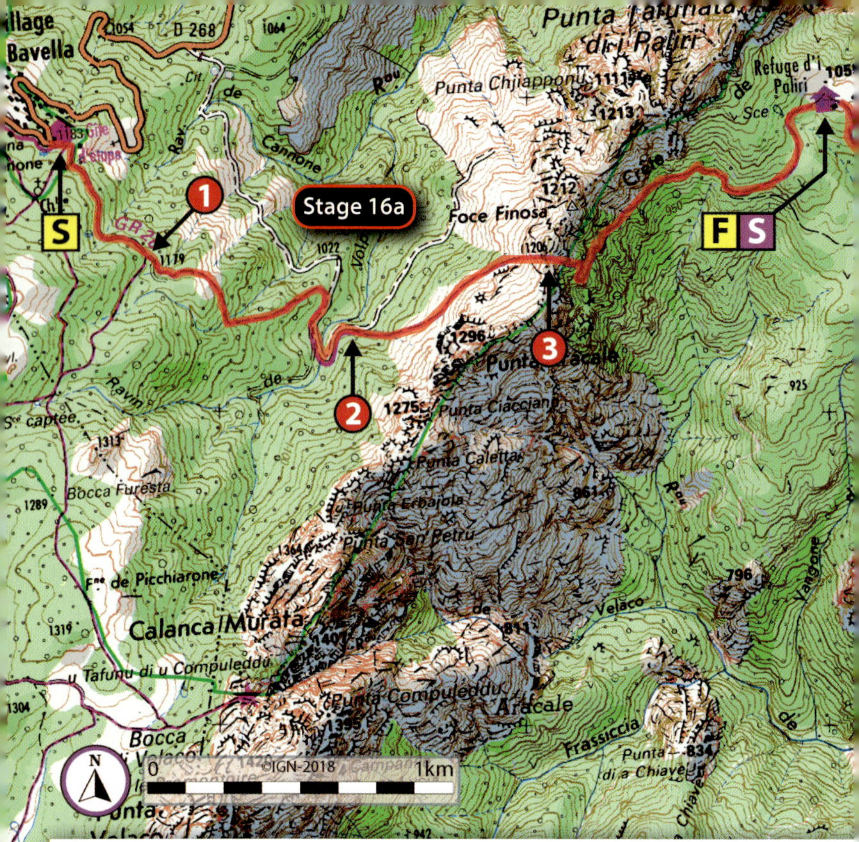

A fixed tent at Refuge d'I Paliri

16a
Monte Bracciutu
Foce di u Bracciu
Bocca di Monte Bracciutu
Stage 16b
GR20
1
Bocca di u Sordu
Punta di Monte Sordu
Monte Sordu
Capellu
di l'Anima Damnata
Crête de Cervu
1054
1091
1064
1016
1020
917
971
911
974
808
858
1117
1065
1041
1113
1096
1053
854
784
761
811
653
955
1091
362
492
594

16a

Approaching Refuge d'I Paliri

N-S

S **See Map 16a**. From the fountain in Bavella, head E on a small road. Shortly afterwards, TR on a track, heading through forest.

1 0:10: Ignore a path on the right (with red waymarks) and continue SH on the track. Shortly afterwards, TL and descend on a path. Soon, descend more steeply over roots. Bear right at a junction, taking the lower of two paths to the right: continue descending.

2 0:25: A few minutes later, TR onto a path and climb.

3 1:00: Cross a pass, **Foce Finosa (1206m)**, and descend steeply. 30min later, start to climb again over roots and rocks. 10min later, pass a source: fill up as there is no source at the refuge itself.

F 1:45: Shortly afterwards, arrive at **Refuge d'I Paliri (1055m)**.

S-N

F **See Map 16a.** From Refuge d'I Paliri, head W on a path. After a few minutes, pass a source. Then descend over roots and rocks. 5-10min later, start to climb.

3 1:10: Cross a pass, **Foce Finosa (1206m)**. Then descend steeply.

2 1:30: TL onto a broad path. After a hairpin bend, ignore a path on the right. Shortly afterwards, TL on a path and climb.

1 1:50: TR on a track. Shortly afterwards, ignore a path on the left.

S 2:00: TL on a small road. Just afterwards, arrive at **Village de Bavella (1180m)** which has a gîte, restaurant, sandwich bar and shop.

Village de Bavella to Refuge d'I Paliri

16a

The view at Foce Finosa

Descend through forest, enjoying tantalising glimpses of the mountains through the trees. After a short, steep climb cross the pass known as Foce Finosa. Finally, another descent, more open this time, leads to the final refuge of the GR20: it is set on a hill so the mountain views over the tree-tops are excellent.

The stage is well marked and navigation is straightforward. The path is mostly well-defined. However, there are some rocky sections and the climb is steep.

	N-S	S-N
Time	1:45	2:00
Distance (km)	4.8	4.8
Ascent (m)	231	359
Descent (m)	359	231
Max Alt (m)	1206	1206

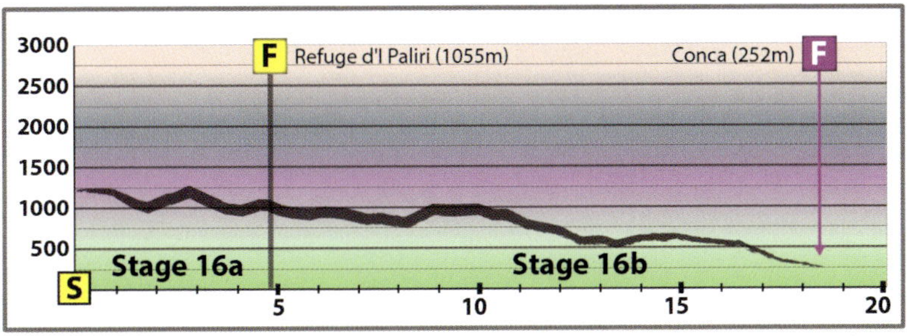

Water: source just before Refuge d'I Paliri

Supplies/Meals: Refuge d'I Paliri

Accommodation: Refuge d'I Paliri

16b
Stage 16b
FORÊT TERRITORIALE DE L'OSPEDALE
©IGN-2018
1km
Punta Pinzuta
Femina Morta
Alive
Antaga
Punta Radichella
Punta di Pusu
MASSIF DE SAN MARTINU
Alzu di Lanu
Bocca d'Usciolu
Punta d'Orlu
Carpiccia
Contra Murata
Conca
Forêt de Valdu
Punta di Cinaja
FORÊT TERRITORIALE DE L'OSPEDALE
MASSIF D'ALBARELLU
Castagna
Poggio di u Pinu
Costa di u Pergulu
Petra Stretta
Bruscaju
CONCA
Arrivée du "G.R.20"
Vous voici au terme
de vôtre odysée.
Vous avez parcouru
environ 180 Km.
Bravo!

Refuge d'I Paliri to Conca

16b

It is a long descent into Conca where the GR20 terminates. The scenery is magnificent to the end. In the low light of early morning, the mountains here take on a wonderful amber colour. On the latter sections of the stage, there are views of the Mediterranean Sea and you should also see the town of Porto-Vecchio.

The lower altitude means that the vegetation is different from the rest of the GR20: you will see Corsica's famous maquis for the first time since Stage 1. You should smell the wild lavender which grows beside the path.

The stage is well marked and navigation is straightforward. The path is mostly well-defined. However, there are some rocky sections. Although the stage is mostly downhill, it seems tiring. There are 1200m of descent and your legs will feel it at the end of this long trek. That said, there are two uphill sections: these are short and not difficult compared to the GR20's other climbs but they seem to suck the energy from your legs. Perhaps this is psychological with your mind realising that you are approaching the end of a challenging undertaking. But no doubt the heat has a part to play too: as you drop to lower elevations, the trail gets hotter and you tire more quickly. It pays to start early.

Water: source at Waypoint No.4; refreshments available in Conca

Supplies/Meals: Conca

Accommodation: Conca

Escape/Access: see 'Travel to/from Trail-heads'

	N-S	S-N
Time	5:15	6:30
Distance (km)	13.6	13.6
Ascent (m)	399	1202
Descent (m)	1202	399
Max Alt (m)	1055	1055

Conca is not far away now!

N-S

S **See Map 16a**. Follow waymarks through the camp-ground. Then descend on a path. Afterwards, a level path heads through forest. After a while, climb steeply over rocks (no waymarks).

1 1:40: 25min later, cross **Bocca di u Sordu (1065m)**. Shortly afterwards, follow waymarks across slabs. Afterwards, a long descent begins.

2 3:10: **See Map 16b**. Cross a stream: there is a popular rock-pool just to the right. Just afterwards, climb quite steeply for 20min. The route then undulates for a while.

3 4:20: Pass through a gap in some rocks, **Bocca d'Usciolu (587m)**, and then descend. The buildings of Conca soon appear below.

4 4:55: Cross a bridge: there is a nearby source. Shortly afterwards, TL onto a road and follow waymarks down through buildings. Eventually, arrive at a T-junction beside Bar du GR20 in **Conca (252m)**: just on the right is the much-photographed plaque claiming to be the finish of the GR20. TL along a road. After a grocery store, TR and descend on another road.

F 5:15: Shortly after the chapel, arrive at **Gîte la Tonnelle** on the left. Congratulations on completing the GR20!

16b

S-N

F **See Map 16b.** From Gîte la Tonnelle, head N on the road. Near the chapel, TR at a fork. TL at a T-junction and pass a grocery store. Just before Bar du GR20, TR on a road and climb.

4 0:30: Leave the road for a path. Shortly afterwards, cross a bridge: there is a nearby source. Continue climbing.

3 1:40: Pass through a gap in some rocks, **Bocca d'Usciolu (587m)**, and then descend. The route then undulates for a while. Later, descend steeply.

2 2:45: Cross a stream: there is a rock-pool just to the left. Afterwards, climb again. **See Map 16a**. After a while, follow waymarks across slabs.

1 4:50: Soon afterwards, cross **Bocca di u Sordu (1065m)**: descend steeply over rocks (no waymarks). Now the path undulates, generally climbing.

S 6:30: Arrive at **Refuge d'I Paliri (1055m)**.

KNIFE EDGE Outdoor Guidebooks